W9-AQJ-533

DISCARD

MILFORD PUBLIC LIBRARY

JEWELRY WITH A HOOK

RECEIVED

SEP 02 2008

JEWELRY WITH A HOOK

CROCHETED FIBER NECKLACES, BRACELETS & MORE

TERRY TAYLOR

LARK BOOKS

A Division of Sterling Publishing Co., Inc.
New York / London

Editor: Julie Hale

Art Director: Dana Irwin

Cover Designer: Cindy LaBreacht

Technical Editor: Karen Manthey

Art Production Assistant: Jeff Hamilton

Illustrator: Orrin Lundgren

Photographer: Stewart O'Shields

Library of Congress Cataloging-in-Publication Data

Taylor, Terry.
  Hooked on jewelry : crocheted fiber necklaces, bracelets, and more / Terry Taylor. -- 1st ed.
    p. cm.
  Includes index.
  ISBN-13: 978-1-60059-016-0 (hc-plc with jacket : alk. paper)
  ISBN-10: 1-60059-016-0 (hc-plc with jacket : alk. paper)
  1. Crocheting--Patterns. 2. Fiberwork. 3. Jewelry making. I. Title.
  TT825.T4 2007
  746.43'4041--dc22

                                                              2007003575

10 9 8 7 6 5 4 3 2 1

First Edition

Published by Lark Books, A Division of
Sterling Publishing Co., Inc.
387 Park Avenue South, New York, N.Y. 10016

Text © 2007, Lark Books
Photography © 2007, Lark Books unless otherwise specified
Illustrations © 2007, Lark Books unless otherwise specified

Distributed in Canada by Sterling Publishing,
c/o Canadian Manda Group, 165 Dufferin Street
Toronto, Ontario, Canada M6K 3H6

Distributed in the United Kingdom by GMC Distribution Services,
Castle Place, 166 High Street, Lewes, East Sussex, England BN7 1XU

Distributed in Australia by Capricorn Link (Australia) Pty Ltd.,
P.O. Box 704, Windsor, NSW 2756 Australia

The written instructions, photographs, designs, patterns, and projects in this volume are intended for the personal use of the reader and may be reproduced for that purpose only. Any other use, especially commercial use, is forbidden under law without written permission of the copyright holder.

Every effort has been made to ensure that all the information in this book is accurate. However, due to differing conditions, tools, and individual skills, the publisher cannot be responsible for any injuries, losses, and other damages that may result from the use of the information in this book.

If you have questions or comments about this book, please contact:
Lark Books, 67 Broadway, Asheville, NC 28801
(828) 253-0467

Manufactured in China

All rights reserved

ISBN 13: 978-1-60059-016-0
ISBN 10: 1-60059-016-0

For information about custom editions, special sales, premium and corporate purchases, please contact Sterling Special Sales Department at 800-805-5489 or specialsales@sterlingpub.com.

This book is for lovers
of fiber, fashionistas,
jewelry enthusiasts
and, oh yes, crocheters.
Grab a hook and
adorn yourselves!

JEWE[LRY]

with a Hook

Introduction 8

Bedeck the Neck

Adorn the Hand & Wrist

ELRY

Lobes and Lapels

Crochet Basics

Introduction

The craft of crochet offers

almost limitless possibilities in terms of color, texture, shape, and design. Contemporary crocheters have discovered that it's an ideal medium for making both flat and dimensional pieces. So why not exploit its versatility to create stylish fiber jewelry?

To show you how to do just that, we've put together a collection of 40 innovative projects created by a group of talented designers. If you're looking to explore new horizons with your crochet hook and favorite fiber, then *Jewelry with a Hook* is the book for you.

Flip through these pages, and you'll be astonished by the diversity of crocheted accessories. There are delicate chokers and ingenious rings, glittering beaded brooches and bold cuffs, all exquisitely executed in a variety of styles and fibers. Along with traditional pieces, you'll find plenty of surprises: a futuristic wristlet made from flexible monofilament; bangle bracelets covered in crocheted cable cording (the kind used in upholstery projects); a dramatic Irish crochet collar featuring dragon and rose motifs. The pieces range from classic to fashion-forward to just plain fun, and they're easier to make than you think. All you need is a hook, some yarn, and basic crochet skills, plus a few jewelry-making supplies that you probably already have on hand.

If you're new to crochet, don't worry—our projects are a snap to complete. Everything you need to know about materials, tools, and techniques can be found in our basics chapter at the back of the book. This section covers the fundamentals of crochet, providing illustrated instructions on how to make the stitches used in each piece. It also offers a run-down of the basic jewelry-making procedures you'll need to know in order to complete our fabulous projects. And remember, ease comes with experience, so you may want to begin with something simple, like our pretty single-crochet Modular Pendants, then move on to a more intricate project, like the opulent Beaded Tapestry Cuff.

Don't be afraid to experiment along the way! Try substituting fibers of different colors and textures for the ones used by our designers. Play around with pretty details—add an extra button, more beads, a bit of fringe. You can easily customize each piece in this book, so that the jewelry you crochet complements your wardrobe and matches your moods. With so many terrific projects to choose from, your biggest challenge will be deciding where to begin. We've included quick little pieces that can be produced in an afternoon, along with more involved projects that will take longer to complete.

Crochet has never been fresher or more fashionable than it is today. So pick out a project, grab a hook and some yarn, and get stitching. Before you know it, your jewelry box will be brimming with beautiful new crocheted fiber accessories.

the
PROJECTS

On the pages that follow, you'll find 40 easy,
innovative crochet jewelry projects.
No matter what your mood—
dramatic, playful, or sophisticated—
there's an accessory for you.

BEDECK THE NECK

Necklaces . Chokers . Pendants

Garden Tapestry Choker

a pretty pattern worked in green with violet accents makes this choker fresh and feminine—just the thing if you're in the mood for spring.

DESIGNER · JESSICA SCHLEICHER

SKILL LEVEL

Intermediate

FINISHED MEASUREMENTS

Directions are given for length of 14"/35.5cm (adjustable up to 18"/45.5cm)

YOU WILL NEED

Approx 20yd/19m size 10 crochet cotton in linen (A)

Approx 12yd/11m size 10 crochet cotton in green (B)

Approx 12-25yd/11-23m size 10 crochet cotton in frosty green (C)

Approx 3yd/2.8m size 10 crochet cotton in lavender (D)

Hook: size 1.5mm/7

2 silver lobster clasps, 5mm

2 silver jump rings, 5mm diameter

Violet sewing thread

Sewing needle

STITCHES USED

Chain stitch (ch)

Slip stitch (sl st)

Single crochet (sc)

GAUGE

11 sts and 10 rows sc = 1"/2.5cm

PATTERN NOTES

How to follow the chart below: Each square counts as 1 sc. The first row of the necklace is also the first row of the graph. Read all odd-numbered rows from right to left, and all even-numbered rows from left to right. Don't carry your thread behind your work, as this will make the necklace uneven and thick. Use a separate section of thread for each color section. Xs on the chart are for flower placement only.

To change color: Work sc in first color until 2 loops remain on hook, yo with 2nd color, yo, draw yarn through 2 loops on hook. Carry all of the loose ends on the WS of the work. These will be woven into the necklace later.

CHOKER FRONT

With A, ch 15.

Row 1: Sc in 2nd ch from hook, sc in each ch from hook, turn - 14 sc.

Rows 2–60: Ch 1, sc in each sc across following chart for color changes, turn - 14 sc. Fasten off.

BORDER AND CHAINS

Changes for neck sizes are as follows in parentheses: 14 (15, 16, 17, 18)"/35.5 (38, 40.5, 43, 45.5) cm.

With B, string the two lobster clasps and the two jump rings onto the thread.

With the RS of choker facing you, join strung B cotton in the top right-hand corner of the choker, ch 1, ★★work 60 sc evenly space across the long edge of choker; working across side edge of choker, ★sc in next st on side edge, ch 25 (33, 41, 49, 57), draw up clasp close to work, ch 1 to lock in place, ch 1 more, sc in 2nd ch from hook and through clasp, sc in next 25 (33, 41, 49, 57) ch, sc in each of next 6 sts on side edge of choker, ch

25 (33, 41, 49, 57), sl st in clasp at end of first tie, ch 1, sc in sl st and the clasp, sc next 25 (33, 41, 49, 57) ch; rep from ★ once, ending in last st on side edge, rep from ★★ once, attaching 2 jump rings on other side edge instead of clasps. Fasten off. Weave in ends.

FLOWER *(make 2)*

With D, ch 4, sl st first ch to form a ring.

Rnd 1: Ch 1, 8 sc in ring, sl st in first sc to join - 8 sc.

Rnd 2: Ch 3, sl st in each sc around, ending with sl st in first sc to join - 8 ch-3 loops. Fasten off. Weave in ends.

FINISHING

Use the sewing needle and the D thread to sew the flowers onto the choker.

This project was created with

1 ball each of *Aunt Lydia's Classic Crochet Cotton*, size 10 in Linen (#21) (A), Myrtle Green (#484) (B), Frosty Green (#661) (C), and Wood Violet (#495) (D), 350yd/320m.

CHART KEY
□ = sc in A
▨ = sc in B
☒ = placement of flower

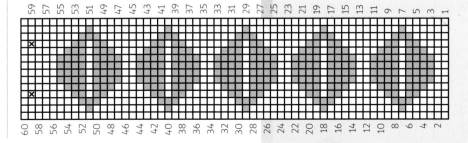

Bountiful Beads Collar

Whether you're dressed up or down, these fabulous felted beads will put the finishing touch on your look. The beads are a snap to crochet and easy to felt.

SMALL BEAD

(make 24 with A,
18 with B, and 18 with C)

Ch 2, 4 sc in 2nd ch from hook, carefully remove hook from last loop, insert hook into top of first sc and into the loop, pull loop through the sc. Fasten off. Double knot beg and ending tails. Weave in ends.

MEDIUM BEAD

(make 28 with A, 23 with B, and 9 with C)

Ch 3, 5-dc puff st in 3rd ch from hook, sl st in top of beg ch. Fasten off. Double knot beg and ending tails. Weave in ends.

LARGE BEAD *(28 with A and 35 with B)*

Ch 4, 8-tr puff st in 4th ch from hook, sl st in top of beg ch. Fasten off. Double knot beg and ending tails. Weave in ends.

FINISHING

Following the instructions on page 123, felt the beads in the washing machine. Then rinse the beads with cold water and wrap them in a towel. Press down on the towel to squeeze out any excess water and spread the beads out on a flat surface so they can dry. If necessary, roll the beads between your fingers to create perfectly round spheres. The beads should be dry in one to two days.

Tip: Twist the felted bead slightly when inserting one of the headpins. A starter hole can be created with a tapestry needle to make inserting the headpin easier.

Insert one of the headpins through a bead. If necessary, trim the end of the headpin with the wire cutters so that it is approximately ½"/13mm long. Use the round-nose pliers to bend the headpin to a right angle. Curl the end of the headpin into a circle so that it meets the right angle of the wire. Before closing the wire completely, place it through one of the links in the chain. Then close the headpin with round-nose pliers to secure it.

Repeat the assembly instructions for the entire necklace, placing the beads on the chain randomly. Many of the links will have two beads attached to them. Depending on how they are arranged, more beads may be needed to sufficiently cover the chain.

Use the needle-nose and the round-nose pliers to open the jump ring at one end of the chain, then slide on the clasp. Close the jump ring. Attach the other half of the clasp to the opposite end of the chain in the same fashion.

This project was created with

1 hank of Cascade Yarns *Cascade 220* (#7829) in dark rust, 100% Peruvian Highland Wool, #4 medium, 3.5oz/100g = 220yd/201m

1 hank of Cascade Yarns *Cascade 220* (#9463) in light rust, 100% Peruvian Highland Wool, #4 medium, 3.5oz/100g = 220yd/201m

1 hank of Cascade Yarns *Cascade 220* (#9429) in olive green, 100% Peruvian Highland Wool, #4 medium, 3.5oz/100g = 220yd/201m.

SKILL LEVEL

Intermediate

FINISHED MEASUREMENTS

Approx 18"/45.5cm long

YOU WILL NEED

95yd/87m medium weight wool yarn (A)

94yd/86m medium weight wool yarn (B)

27yd/24.5m medium weight wool yarn (C)

Hook: size 3.75mm/F-5

183 long gold headpins, each 1"/2.5cm

Tapestry needle

Wire cutters

Round-nose pliers

18"/45.5cm gold cable chain

Gold magnetic clasp

Needle-nose pliers

STITCHES USED

Chain stitch (ch)

Slip stitch (sl st)

Single crochet (sc)

5-dc puff st: (Yo, insert hook in next st, yo, draw yarn through st, yo, draw yarn through 2 loops on hook) 5 times in same st, yo, draw yarn through 6 loops on hook.

8-tr puff st: (Yo twice, insert hook in next st, yo, draw yarn through st, [yo, draw yarn through 2 loops on hook] twice) 8 times in same st, yo, draw yarn through 9 loops on hook.

GAUGE

Exact gauge is not crucial for this project.

Gold & Ruby Choker

all it takes is a few simple stitches to produce this classic choker. The romantic floral motif, set against a background of glittering gold leaves, gives the piece old-fashioned appeal.

SKILL LEVEL

Intermediate

FINISHED MEASUREMENTS

Approx 13½"/34.5cm long

YOU WILL NEED

Approx 28yd/26m #5 cotton thread in red (A)

Approx 9yd/8.5m 6-strand embroidery floss in gold metallic (B)

Hook: size 2mm/3

Tape measure or ruler

2 gold buttons, each ½"/1.3cm

Sewing needle

Sewing thread in gold

STITCHES USED

Chain stitch (ch)

Slip stitch (sl st)

Single crochet (sc)

Half double crochet (hdc)

Double crochet (dc)

Treble crochet (tr)

Picot: Ch 4, sc in 4th ch from hook.

GAUGE

With A, in neck band pattern, 3 rows and width = 1"/2.5cm. With A, flower = 1½"/3.8cm in diameter. With B, in leaf pattern, 7 sc = 1"/2.5cm.

NECK BAND

With A, ch 11.

Row 1: (4 dc, ch 2, 4 dc) in 8th ch from hook, ch 1, skip next 2 ch, dc in last ch, turn.

Row 2: Ch 4 (counts as dc, ch 1), skip next 4 dc, (4 dc, ch 2, 4 dc) in next ch-2 space, ch 1, skip next ch of turning ch, dc in next ch of turning ch, turn.

Rep Row 2 for 37 rows or until neck band measures 13½"/34.5cm from beg or desired length.

Last Row: Ch 1, sc in first dc, sc in next ch-1 space, sc in each of next 4 dc, 5 sc in next ch-2 space, sc in each of next 4 dc, 2 sc in turning ch. Fasten off. Weave in ends.

FLOWER

With A, ch 5, sl st in first ch to form a ring.

Rnd 1: Ch 1, 10 sc in ring, sl st in first sc to join – 10 sc.

Rnd 2: Ch 1, (sc, hdc, dc, tr, picot, tr, dc, hdc, sc) in first sc, skip next sc, ★(sc, hdc, dc, tr, picot, tr, dc, hdc, sc) in next sc, skip next sc; rep from ★ around, sl st in first sc to join. Fasten off. Weave in ends.

LEAF *(make 2)*

With B, ch 15.

Rnd 1: Sc in 2nd ch from hook, sc in each of next 12 ch, 3 sc in last ch for tip, working across opposite side of foundation ch, sc in each of next 13 ch, sc in turning ch, do not join, do not turn.

Work now progresses in rows.

Row 2: Sc in back loop of each of next 10 sc, turn.

Row 3: Ch 1, working in back loops of sts, sc in each of next 10 sc, (sc, ch 1, sc) in next sc for base, sc in each of next 10 sc, turn.

Row 4: Ch 1, working in back loops of sts, sc in each of next 11 sc, (sc, ch 1, sc) in next ch-1 space, sc in each of next 7 sc, turn.

Row 5: Ch 1, working in back loops of sts, sc in each of next 8 sc, (sc, ch 1, sc) in next ch-1 space, sl st in each of next 12 sc. Fasten off. Weave in ends.

FINISHING

Use the gold sewing thread to sew the leaves to the neckband, making sure the tips of the leaves are facing out and that the base of the leaves touch at the center of the neckband. Sew the flower over the center of the leaves, sewing only into the back of the flower petals, so that gold thread does not show on the front of the choker. Press the choker flat using a doubled pressing cloth on top of the choker and setting the iron on warm (not hot). Do not touch the metallic yarn directly with the iron. Sew one button on top of the flower and the other button onto the beg end of the band, using ch-2 space at the end of the choker for the button hole.

This project was created with

1 skein of DMC *Perle Cotton #5* in Ruby (#915) (A), 100% mercerized cotton, 27.3yd/25m.

2 skeins of Presencia *Mouline Especial 6-Strand Embroidery Floss* in Gold (#0009), 35% metallic polyester, 65% viscose, 8.75yd/8m.

Disc-O Necklace

this exuberant necklace is easy to make. Use puka discs or buttons for the colorful rounds, then connect them with a chain of simple stitches. Extra-long, extra-fabulous, the piece can be draped around the neck in a triple strand or layered to create a choker effect.

DESIGNER · **PAULA GRON**

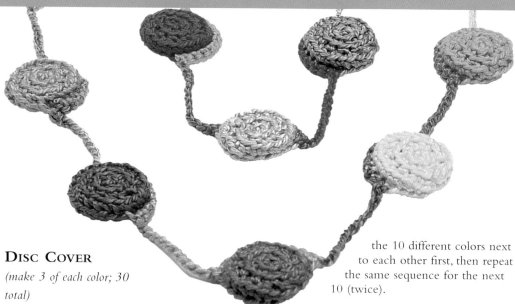

DISC COVER

(make 3 of each color; 30 total)

Ch 4, sl st in first ch to join into a ring.

Rnd 1: Ch 1, work 6 sc in ring, sl st in back loop of first sc to join — 6 sc.

Rnd 2: Working in back loops only, 2 sc in each sc around, sl st in back loop of first sc to join — 12 sc.

Rnd 3: Working in back loops only, ★sc in next sc, 2 sc in next sc; rep from ★ around, sl st in back loop of first sc to join — 18 sc.

Rnd 4: Working in back loops only, ★sc in each of next 2 sc, 2 sc in next sc; rep from ★ around, sl st in back loop of first sc to join — 24 sc.

Rnd 5: Insert the button or disc (hiding the beginning thread end), working in back loops only, ★sc in next sc, skip next sc; rep from ★ around, sl st in back loop of first sc to join — 12 sc.

Rnd 6: Rep Rnd 5 — 6 sc. Fasten off. Weave in ends.

CONNECTING DISCS

Set up the discs in rotation so as not to place the same two colors next to each other. Place the 10 different colors next to each other first, then repeat the same sequence for the next 10 (twice).

Choose a color unlike the first disc while leaving a 6"/15cm tail to begin, ch 12, ★6 sc in visible front loops around one side of the next disc. Lay down a strand of the next color in the established color sequence. Working over the strand of the new color, sc in each of next 6 sc on the same disc; drop the first color, pick up the added-in color and ch 12; cut the dropped color, leaving 3"/7.5cm tails; rep from ★ until all 10 discs are connected; rep from ★ in the same color sequence until 19 discs are connected; sc around the last disc as per pattern but pick up the tail end of the first disc to add-in and cover with the last 6 sc, without twisting the necklace, sl st in first ch at beginning of necklace to join. Fasten off. Weave in the ends.

This project was created with

1 skein each of DMC #3 *Pearl Cotton* thread in Delft Blue (#798 DK), Violet (#552 MD), Tangerine (#743 LT), Burnt Orange (#947), Copper (#920 MD), Plum (#915 DK), Lavender (#210 MD), Blue Green (#502), Electric Blue (#996 MD), and Dusty Rose (#961 DK), 100% cotton, 16yd/14.5m.

SKILL LEVEL

Easy

FINISHED MEASUREMENTS

One size fits most: 2.5yd/2m

YOU WILL NEED

#3 cotton thread weight yarn in 10 different colors of your choice

Hook: size 1.65mm/7

30 flat buttons or puka discs, each 3/4"/2cm

Stitch markers

STITCHES USED

Chain stitch (ch)

Single crochet (sc)

Slip stitch (sl st)

GAUGE

Exact gauge is not crucial to this pattern. First 3 rnds of Disc cover = ¾"/2cm

PATTERN NOTES

The rounds on these discs are worked continuous. When working sl st and sc, work in back loops only. Use stitch markers to mark the beginning of rounds. For ease of handling, when closing over the disc with the stitches, hold the disc instead of the work.

Irish Crochet Collar

ot for the timid, but the results are well worth the time and effort. This ultra-refined collar modernizes traditional Irish crochet motifs. The dragon and rose designs are offset by a cool lace-up closure.

PANEL FRAME *(make 2)*

Ch 152, and without twisting ch, sl st in first ch to form a ring. (Note: Ch should measure approx 13"/33cm long.)

Row 1: Ch 1, sc in each ch around, sl st in first sc to join — 152 sc.

Row 2: Ch 5 (counts as dc, ch 2), skip first sc, skip next sc, ★dc in next sc, ch 2, skip next sc★; rep from ★ to ★ 9 times, (dc, ch 2, dc, ch 2) in next sc, skip next sc; rep from ★ to ★ 4 times, (dc, ch 2, dc, ch 2) in next sc, skip next sc; rep from ★ to ★ 16 times, (dc, ch 2, dc, ch 2) in next sc, skip next sc; rep from ★ to ★ 4 times; (dc, ch 2, dc, ch 2) in next sc, skip next sc; rep from ★ to ★ 10 times, (dc, ch 2, dc, ch 2) in next sc, skip next sc; rep from ★ to ★ 4 times, (dc, ch 2, dc, ch 2) in next sc, skip next sc; rep from ★ to ★ 16 times, (dc, ch 2, dc, ch 2) in next sc, skip next sc; rep from ★ to ★ 4 times, dc in first sc, same place as starting ch-5, ch 2, sl st in 3rd ch of beginning ch — 84 ch-2 spaces.

Row 3: Ch 1, ★2 sc in each of next 3 ch-2 spaces, turn, (ch 6, skip next 2 sc, sc in next sc) twice, turn, 7 sc in next ch-6 loop, 4 sc in next ch-6 loop, ch 6, turn, skip next 7 sc, sc in next sc, turn, (3 sc, ch 3, 3 sc, ch 3, 3 sc) in next ch-6 loop, 3 sc in next ch-6 loop already holding 4 sc★; rep from ★ to ★ 4 times, making 5 edging motifs, ★★2 sc in each of next 3 ch-2 spaces, turn, ch 6, skip next 4 sc, sc in next sc, turn, (3 sc, ch 3, 3 sc, ch 3, 3 sc) in next ch-6 loop★★, 2 sc in each of next 18 ch-2 spaces, rep from ★★ to ★★ 8 times, 2 sc in each of next 18 ch-2 spaces, rep from ★★ to ★★ once, rep from ★ to ★ once, sl st in first sc to join. Fasten off. Weave in ends.

ROSE *(make 2)*

Ch 6, sl st in first ch to form a ring.

Rnd 1: (Ch 3, sc) 7 times in ring, do not join — 7 ch-3 loops. Work in a spiral. Mark first st of each rnd, moving marker up as work progresses.

Rnd 2: (Ch 3, sc) in each loop around — 7 ch-3 loops.

Rnd 3: (Sc, ch 5, sc) in each ch-3 loop around — 7 ch-5 loops.

Rnd 4: (Sc, 5 dc, sc) in each ch-5 loop around — 7 petals.

Work now progresses in rows.

Row 5: Sc in each of next 5 sts, ★ch 4, skip next 4 sts, sc in each of next 3 sts; rep from ★ 3 times, turn — 4 ch-4 loops.

Row 6: ★Skip next sc, sc in next sc, 7 dc in next ch-4 loop; rep from ★ 3 times, skip next st, sc in next sc, turn — 4 petals.

Work now progresses in rnds.

Rnd 7: Ch 5, skip next 3 sts, sc in each of next 3 sts, ★ch 5, skip next 5 sts, sc in each of next 3 sts; rep from ★ twice, ch 7, skip next 2 sts, sc in next sc, ★ch 7, skip next 6 sts in Rnd 4, sc in next st; rep from ★ once, ch 7, skip next 6 sts in next sc, do not join. Work in a spiral as before.

Rnd 8: ★(Sc, 10 dc, sc) in next ch-5 loop, skip next sc, sc in next sc; rep from ★ 3 times, (sc, 8 dc, sc) in each of next 4 ch-7 loops, sl st in first sc to join. Fasten off. Weave in ends.

SKILL LEVEL

Experienced

FINISHED MEASUREMENTS

6"/15cm x 11½"/29cm

YOU WILL NEED

250yd/229m size 10 crochet cotton in black

Hook: size 1.7mm/5

24 black rubber O-rings or metal jump rings with a soldered joint, ½"/1.3cm diameter

Tapestry needle

STITCHES USED

Chain stitch (ch)

Single crochet (sc)

Double crochet (dc)

GAUGE

Exact gauge is not crucial to this pattern. 12 sts = 1"/2.5cm.

LEAF WITHOUT A STEM (make 2)

Ch 19.

Row 1: Dc in 4th ch from hook, ★ch 1, skip next ch, dc in next ch; rep from ★ 6 times, dc in last ch, turn — 7 ch-1 spaces.

Row 2: Ch 1, ★skip next ch-1 space, 5 dc in next dc, skip next ch-1 space, sc in next dc; rep from ★ twice, skip next ch-1 space, 5 dc in next dc, (sc, ch 2, sc) in ch-3 loop at end of Row 1, working across opposite side of foundation ch, 5 dc in next ch at base of dc, ★★skip next ch, sc in next ch, skip next ch, 5 dc in next ch; rep from ★★ twice, skip next ch, sc in next ch. Fasten off.

LEAF WITH A STEM (make 2)

Work same as the leaf without a stem, do not fasten off at end of Row 2.

Stem: Ch 10, sc in 2nd ch from hook, sc in each of next 8 ch. Fasten off. Sew end of stem to end of one leaf without a stem. Rep with other two leaves.

DRAGON

Ch 54.

Row 1: Sc in 6th ch from hook, ★ch 1, skip next ch, dc in next ch; rep from ★14 times, ch 1, skip next ch, sc in next ch, turn, leaving remaining ch sts unworked — 16 ch-1 spaces.

Work now progresses in rnds.

Rnd 2: 2 sc in first ch-1 space, 3 dc in each of next 6 ch-1 spaces, 2 dc in each of next 5 ch-1 spaces, dc in each of next 4 ch-1 spaces, 10 dc in next ch-5 loop at end of Row 1, working across opposite side of foundation ch, 3 dc in each of next 6 ch-1 spaces, 2 dc in each of next 5 ch-1 spaces, dc in each of next 4 ch-1 spaces, 2 sc in next ch-1 space, skip next ch, sc in each of next 15 ch sts, (sc, ch 5, sc) in last ch (for end of tail), working across opposite side of same ch, sc in each of next 15 ch, do not join. Continue to work in a spiral.

Rnd 3: Dc in each of next 40 sts, ch 8, sc in 3rd ch from hook, dc in each of next 5

ch (bottom jaw made), skip next 2 sc, sc in each of next 2 dc in Rnd 2, ch 8, sc in 3rd ch from hook, dc in each of next 5 ch (top jaw made), skip next 2 sc, ★sc in each of next 3 sts in Rnd 2, ch 3; rep from ★ across to ch-5 loop at end of tail, (3 sc, ch 4, 3 sc) in next ch-5 loop at end of tail, working across top of tail, (sc in next sc, 2 sc in next sc) 8 times.

Work now progresses in a row.

Row 4: ★★Ch 12, (sc, ch 6, sc) in 7th ch from hook, ch 6, sc in next ch, dc in each of next 4 ch (leg made), skip next 2 sts★★, sc in each of next 5 sts; rep from ★★ to ★★, sc in each of next 11 sts; rep from ★★ to ★★, sc in each of next 5 sts; rep from ★★ to ★★, sc in next st. Fasten off. Weave in ends.

CLOVER (make 1 for the end of the dragon's tail)

Ch 5, sl st in first ch to form a ring.

Rnd 1: (Ch 5, sc) 3 times in ring, do not join — 3 ch-5 loops. Work in a spiral.

Rnd 2: (Sc, 8 dc, sc) in each loop around, sl st in first sc to join — 3 petals. Fasten off, leaving a sewing length. Sew Clover to ch-4 loop at end of Dragon's tail.

LACING

Make a 2nd clover, do not fasten off at end of Rnd 2, make a ch at least 2yd/1.8m long so that the piece can be slipped over the head while laced. Make a 3rd clover at the end of the ch. Fasten off. (Note: A shorter ch, 4'/1.2m long can be used, in which case you should lace only the top loops before putting Triptych on, then thread the remaining loops.)

FINISHING

Sew one set of two leaves to each rose (see diagram). Baste the panel frames face down on a firm fabric or pin to a hard pillow, squaring up the sides. Then pin the motifs in the center of the frames.

The backgrounds can be filled in using a ch st or any traditional Irish crochet background, as desired. My piece was done with a single thread pulled randomly from one side of the frame to the motif. A buttonhole stitch was worked over the thread. The thread was then run neatly along the back to the next place, and the process was repeated.

See page 126 for instructions on blocking the pieces. Then sew 6 O-rings or jump rings to the outer edges of the panels. Sew 6 in between the panels, sewing to both sides, using an overhand stitch. Lace the back of the piece.

This project was created with

1 ball of DMC *Traditions* Crochet Cotton Thread, in black (#310),100% mercerized cotton, 320m/350yd.

FIRST ROSE PANEL   DRAGON PANEL   SECOND ROSE PANEL

Jewelry with a Hook

Soft & Simple Choker

t his earthy, easy-to-assemble choker is made from variegated yarn in autumnal hues. Beads in mellow shades of gold and amber add a natural touch to the soft crocheted trim.

DESIGNER · MaryKate Newcomb

SKILL LEVEL

Intermediate

FINISHED MEASUREMENTS

Pendant: Approx 1"/2.5cm wide

Necklace: Approx 12"/30.5cm long

YOU WILL NEED

Approx 100yd/91m worsted weight variegated yarn in green, white, and orange (One skein will produce four or five necklaces.)

Hooks: 3.5mm/E-4 and 1.4mm/8 for pulling yarn through buttonholes/shaft

Seed beads, size E/6 (I used a multi-pack that included amber and yellow glass beads.)

Bead-threading needle

Matching button for closure, ¾"/2cm (I used a vintage button from my collection. Buttons with holes or shafts work well for this project.)

Tapestry needle

STITCHES USED

Chain stitch (ch)

Single crochet (sc)

Slip stitch (sl st)

SPECIAL STITCHES

Beaded chain stitch (BCH): Slide bead up to hook, yo, draw yarn through loop on hook.

3-dc cluster (3-dc CL): (Yo, insert hook in next st, yo, draw yarn through st, yo, draw yarn through 2 loops on hook) 3 times in same st, yo, draw yarn through 4 loops on hook.

3-tr cluster (3-tr CL): (Yo twice, insert hook in next st, yo, draw yarn through st, [yo, draw yarn through 2 loops on hook] twice) 3 times in same st, yo, draw yarn through 4 loops on hook.

GAUGE

Gauge is not crucial to this project, but each pattern repeat for the example is 2"/5cm long. The example has 8½ pattern repeats. Check the length of your starting chain to see if it fits comfortably. If it's too small, add 1 more pattern repeat (string an additional 24 beads and add 11 BCH to foundation ch).

PREPARATION

Practice the pattern without beads on plain cotton crochet thread (size 3 is good) to familiarize yourself with the pattern. It's difficult to rip out mistakes in mohair yarn, so it's best to know the pattern well before using the mohair yarn.

Carefully string about 214 beads onto the mohair yarn (each pattern repeat requires 24 beads; add 24 beads for each additional repeat).

PATTERN

Work 95 BCH or a multiple of 11 for desired length.

Row 1: Ch 10 without beads for button loop, skip next 10 ch, sc in first BCH (button loop formed). Slide most of remaining beads down a few yds, leaving 5-10 close to work, ★3-dc CL in next BCH, ch 1, BCH, ch 1, skip next BCH, 3-tr CL in next BCH, ch 1, BCH 1, ch 1, skip next BCH, 3-dc CL in next BCH, sc in next BCH★★, ch 3, BCH, ch 3, skip next 4 BCH, sc in next BCH; rep from ★ across, ending last rep at ★★, turn.

To attach the button, draw up a loop about 3"/7.5cm long. Using the 9 hook, gently pull the loop through both holes or the shaft of the button, sl st into the last BCH and pull the yarn to tighten the loop.

Row 2: ★Ch 2, BCH, ch 2, skip next BCH, sc in next ch-1 space, work 7 BCH, sc in next ch-1 space, ch 2, BCH, ch 2, sc in next sc★★, ch 4, BCH, ch 4, skip next loop, sc in next sc; rep from ★ across, ending last rep at ★★. Fasten off. Weave in ends.

FINISHING

At the button end of the necklace, thread the yarn end through a needle that's small enough to fit through the buttonhole. Sew in and out of the buttonhole, and into the last sc several times to fasten it securely. Weave in the ends.

This project was created with

1 skein of Alchemy Yarns *Haiku* in Early Fall Colorway, 40% silk, 60% mohair, .875oz/25g = 325yd/297m.

Silver Pendant Wrap

t he perfect way to display a heart-shaped stone, this pretty pendant wrap is delicate yet durable. A crocheted chain of metallic thread holds the heart securely in place.

DESIGNER · ALEXANDRA CALUB

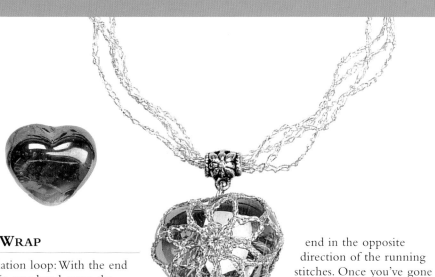

SKILL LEVEL

Intermediate

FINISHED MEASUREMENTS

18"/45.5cm long

YOU WILL NEED

Approximately 12yd/10.8m silver metallic embroidery thread

Hook: 1.25mm/8 steel thread hook

Darning needle or any sharp-pointed needle with an eye to fit thread

Glass heart-shaped stone, 1"/2.5cm wide

3 silver antique-finish pendant bails

3 silver rings, each 5mm diameter

Needle-nose pliers

Silver lobster lock set

STITCHES USED

Chain stitch (ch)

Slip stitch (sl st)

Single crochet (sc)

Double crochet (dc)

GAUGE

Gauge for the necklace is not crucial, as it is dependent on neck size. However, the gauge for the pendant wrap is important. The pattern for the wrap is intended for a stone about 1"/2.5cm wide. Keep in mind that if your stone is too big, it will be difficult to insert into the wrap. If the stone is too small, the wrap will be too loose.

PATTERN NOTES

You will not turn your work. Because the silver thread is thinner than the kind usually used with a size 1.25mm/8 hook, the stitches will naturally be loose.

PENDANT WRAP

Make a foundation loop: With the end of the thread in one hand, wrap the thread around your index fingers and hold the thread where it closes into a circle. Insert the hook into the circle. YO and pull the thread through the circle. Note: If your loop becomes bigger as you work through the wrap, simply tighten it by pulling on the end of the thread.

Rnd 1: Ch 1. Work 16 sc into loop. Sl st to 1st sc.

Rnd 2: (Sc in next sc, ch 5, sk next sc) 7 times. Sc in next sc. Ch 2. Sk next. Dc in 1st sc. — 8 loops (where last dc counts as 1 loop)

Rnd 3: Sc around post of last dc. (Ch 5, Sc in loop) 7 times. Ch 2. Dc in 1st sc.

At this point pull foundation loop tight and weave end in with the darning needle.

Rnd 4: Repeat Rnd 3.

Rnd 5: Sc around post of last dc. (Ch 5, Sc in loop) 7 times. Ch 5. Sl st to 1st sc.

Rnd 6: Ch 1. Work 4 sc in each loop around. — 32 sc.

Fasten off, leaving 7" for sewing. Insert the glass heart stone in the wrap just made with Rnd 1 in the center front of the stone. Use the darning needle to sew running stitches along the last sc round. Pull the thread to tighten the stitches and close the back of the wrap. Use the darning needle to secure the stitches by weaving the end in the opposite direction of the running stitches. Once you've gone all the way around, cut the thread.

FINISHING THE PENDANT

With the stone now wrapped, position any sc on Rnd 4 over the heart's cleft. Use the needle-nose pliers to open one of the silver rings, slip the ring through this sc and through the loop on one of the pendant bails, then close the ring with the pliers. Make sure that the heart is facing front.

MAKING THE CHAIN

Work two chains that are double the neck size you want, fastening off at the end of each chain and leaving 2"/5.5cm of thread at each end for knotting. For example, for a choker with a length of 12"/30.5cm, the chain should be 24"/61cm long.

FINISHING THE FIRST CHOKER END

Insert 2 strands of the chain into one of the pendant bails, then position the bail so that it's in the center of the 2 strands. Fold the strands with the pendant bail at one end, so that you have 4 strands of chain. Make a

knot with the 4 strands to hold the bail in place. With the needle-nose pliers, open one of the silver rings, slip it though the loop on the pendant bail, then close the ring with the pliers.

PLACING THE PENDANT

With the four strands of chain together, insert the unfinished choker end through the pendant bail with the wrapped stone.

FINISHING THE OTHER CHOKER END

Insert 2 strands of the chain into the last pendant bail. Knot the 4 loose ends together and place the bail over the knot. Make a knot with the 4 strands to hold the last bail in place. Use the needle-nose pliers to open the last silver ring, then slip the ring through the loop in the last bail. Add the lobster lock clasp to the silver ring, then close the ring with the pliers.

END NOTES

Try using different stones and different fibers in this project. Stones from your yard will work well with natural fibers like raffia. Stones of any shape can be used. The stone featured in this project was taken from an aquarium set.

If you can't find a suitable pendant bail, use two beads with centers that are big enough to hold the four strands of chains. Place the beads on either side of the wrapped stone attached to the necklace with a silver ring.

To care for your choker, hand-wash it and let it air-dry.

This project was created with

1 spool of Coats *Anchor Ophir* thread in Silver (#301), 60% viscose, 40% metallic polyester, 44yd/40m.

Daisy Chain

DESIGNER · NICOLE TIRONA

Crocheted **b**lossoms

pair up with beads and

chain in this breezy,

easy-to-wear necklace.

SKILL LEVEL

Intermediate

FINISHED MEASUREMENTS

Approx 52"/132cm long

YOU WILL NEED

Approx 10½yd/9.6m bedspread weight cotton thread in yellow (A)

Approx 10yd/9.2m bedspread weight cotton thread in white (B)

Approx 5yd/4.5m bedspread weight cotton thread in kelly green (C)

Hooks: 1.15mm/10 and 3.25mm/D-3

Darning needle or needle with eye to fit thread

15 copper head pins

Needle-nose pliers

10 glass leaf-shaped beads in green,10 x 12mm

30 glass triangle beads in yellow, 2mm

5 mother-of-pearl bird-shaped beads, 18mm

10 luster fire-polished beads, 4mm

Open-linked copper chain, 23–25"/58–60cm

2 copper lobster clasps

2 copper jump rings, 5mm diameter (Optional. If the chain is soldered closed, the jump rings can be used to connect the crochet flowers to the chain.)

Round-nose pliers

STITCHES USED

Chain stitch (ch)

Slip stitch (sl st)

Single crochet (sc)

Half double crochet (hdc)

Double crochet (dc)

Treble crochet (tr)

5-dc puff st: (Yo, insert hook in next st, yo, draw yarn through st, yo, draw yarn through 2 loops on hook) 5 times in same st, yo, draw yarn through 6 loops on hook.

3-trtr puff st: *Yo (4 times), insert hook in next st, yo, draw yarn through st, (draw yarn through 2 loops on hook) 4 times; rep from * twice in same st, yo, draw yarn through 4 loops on hook.

GAUGE

Exact gauge is not crucial for this pattern. With the smaller hook, the posey = 1"/2.5cm in diameter. With the larger hook, the daisy = 1¼"/3.2cm in diameter. With the smaller hook, the small leaf = ¾"/2cm long. With the smaller hook, the large leaf = 1"/2.5cm long.

POSEY *(make 3)*

With the smaller hook and A, make a foundation loop. With the end of the thread in one hand, wrap the thread around your index finger and hold the thread where it closes into a circle. Insert the hook into the circle. Yo and pull the thread through the circle. Note: If your loop becomes bigger as you work through the wrap, simply tighten it by pulling on the end of the thread.

Rnd 1: Ch 1, 12 sc in foundation loop, sl st in first sc to join — 12 sc.

Rnd 2: Ch 1, sc in first sc, 5 dc in next sc, *sc in next sc, 5 dc in next sc; rep from * around, sl st in first sc to join — 6 petals. Fasten off. Tighten foundation loop. Weave in ends.

DAISY *(make 5)*

Center of flower

With larger hook and A, ch 3, 5-dc puff st in 3rd ch from hook.

Rnd 1: Ch 1, work 4 sc around the post of last dc of puff st, sc in base ch, work 4 sc around the ch-2 loop on side of puff st, sc in top of puff st, sl st in first sc to join — 10 sc. Fasten off. Weave in ends.

Petals

Rnd 2: With larger hook, join B with sc in any sc of center, 5 dc in next sc, ★sc in next sc, 5 dc in next sc; rep from ★ around, sl st in first sc to join — 5 petals. Fasten off. Weave in ends.

Small Leaf (make 4)

With smaller hook and C, ch 6, 3-trtr puff st in 6th ch from hook, ch 1 tightly. Fasten off. Weave in ends.

Large Leaf (make 4)

With smaller hook and C, ch 10.

Row 1: Sc in 2nd ch from hook, hdc in next ch, dc in next ch, tr in each of next 2 ch, dc in each of next 2 ch, hdc in next ch, 3 sc in last ch, working across opposite side of foundation ch, hdc in next ch, dc in each of next 2 ch, tr in each of next 2 ch, dc in next ch, hdc in next ch, sc in next ch, sl st in next ch to join. Fasten off. Weave in ends.

ASSEMBLY

Assembled leaf bead (make 10): Use the needle-nose pliers to make a loop in the end of one of the headpins. Then slide one of the leaf beads onto the headpin, followed by 3 of the triangle beads. Set the headpin aside.

Assembled bird bead (make 5): Use the needle-nose pliers to make a loop in the end of one of the headpins. Then slide one of the fire-polished beads onto the headpin, followed by one of the bird beads and one of the fire-polished beads. Set the headpin aside.

Attach one assembled leaf bead to both sides of each daisy, with the triangle beads pointing toward the daisy. Make sure you pick up two threads (or a whole stitch), not just one thread, when poking the open loop of your headpin into the crochet flower or leaf. Use the wire cutters to trim any excess wire from the headpin.

On a clean, flat surface, lay out a piece of blank paper and make a guide for your necklace by measuring 52"/132cm. Arrange the connector charms and crochet leaves

along the guideline, so that the arrangement of beads and crochet leaves is evenly spaced. Try to imagine the long necklace draped — this can aid you in your aesthetic decisions. Remember that the lobster clasps (the beginning and end of the necklace) should be positioned on your chest and not at the back of your neck.

Use the copper chain to connect the charms. Measure the space between two charms/crochet pieces and cut a piece of chain to fit that space. If your copper chain has open links, you can easily open the links with round-nose pliers to attach the chain to the crochet pieces. If your chain links are soldered shut, use jump rings where necessary.

FINISHING

Finish the necklace by using the needle-nose pliers to attach the lobster clasp to both ends. The unique design of the necklace allows you to play with the finished product — you can easily adjust the length or make the piece look like a two-layer necklace.

This project was created with

1 ball each of Coats Manila Bay *Cannon* bedspread weight cotton thread in Yellow (#MB045), White, and Kelly Green (#MB767), 100% mercerized cotton, 185yd/175m.

Icicles Necklace

Like frost glistening on grass, the sheen of this gorgeous necklace makes it a true attention-getter. Crocheted from metallic yarn, it's sophisticated but a snap to make.

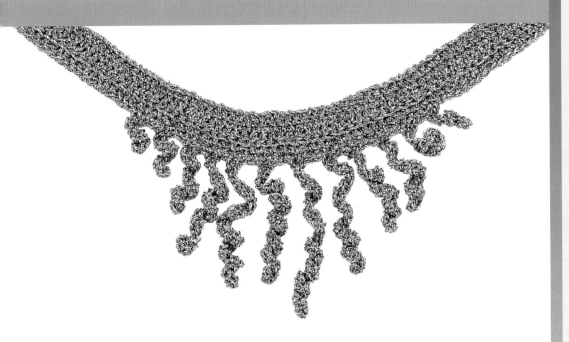

SKILL LEVEL

Easy

FINISHED MEASUREMENTS

16½"/42cm long excluding clasp

YOU WILL NEED

104yd/95m lightweight metallic yarn in pewter

Hook: size 2.75mm/C-2

Tapestry needle

Needle-nose pliers

2 silver jump rings

Silver toggle clasp, 15mm

STITCHES USED

Slip stitch (sl st)

Chain stitch (ch)

Single crochet (sc)

Double crochet (dc)

GAUGE

6 sts and 4 rows sc = 1"/2.5cm

BAND

Ch 100.

Row 1 (WS): Dc in 3rd ch from hook, dc in each ch across, turn 99 sts.

Row 2: Ch 2 (counts as dc), skip first dc, dc in each dc across, dc in top of turning ch, turn.

Row 3: Rep Row 2. Fasten off.

TO MAKE THE ICICLES

Row 4: With RS facing, skip first 33 sts, join yarn in next st, ch 10, sc in 2nd ch from hook, sc in each of next 8 ch, sc in each of next 3 sc on band, ch 15, sc in 2nd ch from hook, sc in each of next 13 ch, sc in each of next 3 sc on band, ch 20, sc in 2nd ch from hook, sc in each of next 18 ch, sc in each of next 3 sc on band, ch 25, sc in 2nd ch from hook, sc in each of next 23 ch, sc in each of next 3 sc on band, ch 30, sc in 2nd ch from hook, sc in each of next 28 ch, sc in each of next 3 sc on band, (ch 35, sc in 2nd ch from hook, sc in each of next 33 ch, sc in each of next 3 sc on band) twice, ch 30, sc in 2nd ch from hook, sc in each of next 28 ch, sc in each of next

3 sc on band, ch 25, sc in 2nd ch from hook, sc in each of next 23 ch, sc in each of next 3 sc on band, ch 20, sc in 2nd ch from hook, sc in each of next 18 ch, sc in each of next 3 sc on band, ch 15, sc in 2nd ch from hook, sc in each of next 13 ch, sc in each of next 3 sc on band, ch 10, sc in 2nd ch from hook, sc in each of next 8 ch, sl st in next sc on band. Fasten off. Weave in ends. The icicles should be slightly curly.

FINISHING

Use the needle-nose pliers to open one of the jump rings and hook the ring onto the first stitch of the first row. Add the toggle loop, then use the needle-nose pliers to close the ring. Use the needle-nose pliers to open the second jump ring, hook the ring onto the last stitch of the first row, then add the toggle and close the ring.

This project was created with

Rowan Lurex *Shimmer* in Pewter, 80% viscose and 20% polyester, 1 3.4oz/50g = 104yd/95m.

Soft & Pink Collar

p lush mohair and boucle yarns in scrumptious shades of pink make this collar lavish. The button closure at the back is a pretty accent.

SKILL LEVEL

Intermediate

FINISHED MEASUREMENTS

16"/41cm circumference

6"/15cm tall

YOU WILL NEED

50yd/46m light worsted weight mohair in pink (A)

25yd/23m cotton/rayon boucle in light pink (B) and burgundy (C)

Hooks: 3.75mm/F-5 and 2mm/3

Yarn needle

Button

Sewing needle

STITCHES USED

Chain stitch (ch)

Single crochet (sc)

Double crochet (dc)

Treble crochet (tr)

2-tr puff st: (Yo twice, insert hook in next st, yo, draw yarn through st, [yo, draw yarn through 2 loops on hook] twice) twice in same st, yo, draw yarn through 3 loops on hook.

GAUGE

In neck band pattern, (sc, ch 5) 4 times = 4"/10cm unstretched.

NECK BAND

With A, ch 66 or a multiple of 4 plus 2 to fit comfortably around neck with ½"/13mm overlap.

Row 1: Sc in 6th ch from the hook, ★ch 5, skip next 3 ch, sc in next ch; rep from ★ across to within last 4 ch, ch 3, skip next 3 ch, dc in last ch, turn — 16 loops.

Row 2: (Ch 5, sc) in each loop across to within last ch-5 loop, ch 3, dc in last ch-5 loop, turn - 16 loops.

Row 3: (Ch 5, sc) in each loop across to last ch-5 loop, sl st in last ch-5 loop — 16 loops. Fasten off. Weave in ends.

FLOWER #1 *(make 1 each with A, B, and C)*

With smaller hook, ch 6, sl st in first ch to form a ring.

Row 1: Ch 1, ★sc in ring, ch 4, 2-tr puff st in ring, ch 4; rep from ★ 4 times, sl st in first sc to join - 5 petals. Fasten off. Weave in ends.

FLOWER #2

With B, ch 5, sl st in first ch to form a ring.

Row 1: Ch 4 (count as dc, ch 1), (dc, ch 1) 9 times in ring, sl st to 3rd ch of beginning ch to join — 10 ch-1 spaces.

RING *(make 1 with larger hook and A, and 1 with smaller hook and B)*

Ch 12, sl st in first ch to form a ring

Row 1: Ch 1, work 18 sc in ring, sl st in first sc to join. Fasten off. Weave in ends.

WHEEL *(make 1 with larger hook and A, and 1 with smaller hook and B)*

Ch 5, sl st in first ch to form a ring

Row 1: Ch 6 (counts as dc, ch 3), (dc, ch 3) 5 times in ring, sl st in 3rd ch of beginning ch to join.

Rnd 2: Ch 1, work 4 sc in each ch-3 loop around, sl st in first sc to join. Fasten off. Weave in ends.

ASSEMBLY

With the yarn needle and matching yarn, sew the pieces to the neck band (see diagram). Then sew the button near the left end of the choker, using ch-5 loop on the opposite end for the button loop.

This project was created with

Yumco's *Lela* (#308), lot #929, 52% cotton, 48% rayon, 3 1/2oz/100g = 265yd/242m

Matrex's Panther Yarns *Dora* (#516), 60% acrylic, 40% mohair, 1.75oz/50g = 136yd/125m

Row 2: Ch 1, sc in first st, ★ 5 dc in next dc★★, sc in next dc; rep from ★ around, ending last rep at ★★, sl st in first sc to join — 5 petals. Fasten off. Weave in ends.

LEAF *(make 3)*

With larger hook and A, ch 10.

Rnd 1: Sc in the 2nd ch from hook, sc in each of next 7 ch, 3 sc in last ch, working across opposite side of foundation ch, sc in each of next 8 ch, sc in turning ch, do not join. Work in a spiral.

Rnd 2: Sc in each of next 9 sc, 2 sc in next sc, sc in each of next 9 sc, 2 sc in next sc, sl st in next sc to join. Fasten off. Weave in ends.

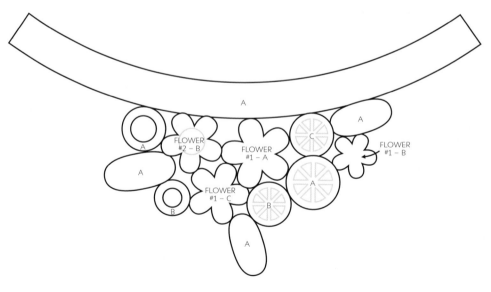

Sculptural Necklace

DESIGNER · **ELIZABETA NEDELJKOVICH-MARTONOSI**

bright colors and a playful pattern —this luxurious necklace has it all. To wear it, simply tie the ends in a loose knot at the back of your neck.

Intermediate

FINISHED MEASUREMENTS

16"/40.5cm in circumference (excluding ties)

6½"/17cm tall

YOU WILL NEED

100yd/92m sport weight yarn in brown (A)

5–10yd/4.5-9.2m worsted weight yarn in brown spotted with olive green (B), dark green (C), light green (D), blue-green (E), ivory (F),

5–10yd/4.5-9.2m sport weight yarn in orange (G), yellow (H),

Hook: size 3.75 mm/F-5

Pillow filler

Yarn needle

STITCHES USED

Chain stitch (ch)

Single crochet (sc)

Slip stitch (sl st)

Treble crochet (tr)

2-tr puff st: (Yo twice, insert hook in next st, yo, draw yarn through st, [yo, draw yarn through 2 loops on hook] twice) twice in same st, yo, draw yarn through 3 loops on hook.

Knot stitch (knot st): Draw up a loop 1"/2.5cm long, yo, draw yarn through long loop on hook (ch made), insert hook in single strand (bottom part) of long loop just made, yo, draw yarn through loop, yo, draw through 2 loops on hook (sc made to complete knot st).

GAUGE

With A, choker = approx ¾"/2cm in diameter. With worsted weight yarn, leaf = 1¼ x 2"/3.2 x 5cm.

CHOKER

With A ch 2.

Rnd 1: Work 7 sc in 2nd ch from hook, do not join — 7 sc. Work in a spiral.

Rnd 2: Sc in each sc around — 7 sc.

Rep Rnd 2 until choker measures 16"/40.5cm or desired length, stuffing with pillow filling after every 1½"/3.8cm.

Last Rnd: *Sc in next sc, skip next sc; rep from * 3 times, sl st in next sc to join.

Fasten off.

TIE BALL (make 2)

With A, ch 2.

Rnd 1: Work 6 sc in 2nd ch from hook, do not join — 6 sc. Work in a spiral.

Rnds 2–6: Sc in each sc around - 7 sc. Stuff with pillow filling before next rnd.

Rnd 7: *Sc in next sc, skip next sc; rep from * 3 times, sl st in next sc to join, ch 32 for Tie. Fasten off, leaving a sewing length. With yarn needle and sewing length, sew end of tie to one end of choker. Rep ball and tie on other end of choker.

LEAF (make 3 with C, 2 with D, and 3 with E)

Ch 10.

Row 1: Sc in 2nd ch from hook, sc in each of next 7 ch, (sc, ch 2, sc) in last ch, working across opposite side of foundation ch, sc in each of next 6 ch, turn.

Row 2: Ch 1, sc in each of first 7 sc, (sc, ch 2, sc) in next ch-2 space, sc in each of next 7 sc, turn.

Row 3: Ch 1, sc in each of next 8 sc, (sc, sl st) in next ch-2 space. Fasten off.

FLOWER

With B, ch 6, sl st in first ch to form a ring.

Rnd 1: Ch 1, *sc in ring, ch 4, 2-tr puff st in ring, ch 4; rep from * 4 times, sl st in first sc to join — 5 petals. Fasten off. Weave in ends.

SMALL RING (make 2 with F and 1 with B)

Ch 8, sl st in first ch to form a ring

Rnd 1: Ch 1, work 12 sc in ring, sl st in first sc to join. Fasten off. Weave in ends.

LARGE RING (make 3 with A)

Ch 10, sl st in first ch to form a ring

Rnd 1: Ch 1, work 16 sc in ring, sl st in first sc to join. Fasten off. Weave in ends.

SMALL DANGLING BALL (make 2)

With G, ch 2.

Rnd 1: Work 6 sc in 2nd ch from hook, do not join — 6 sc. Work in a spiral.

Rnd 2: Work 2 sc in each sc around — 12 sc.

Rnds 3–7: Sc in each sc around — 12 sc. Fill ball before next rnd.

Rnd 8: *Sc in next sc, skip next sc; rep from * 5 times, sl st in next sc to join — 6 sc. Fasten off, leaving a sewing length.

LARGE DANGLING BALL (make 1)

With H, ch 2.

Rnd 1: Work 6 sc in 2nd ch from hook, do not join — 6 sc. Work in a spiral.

Rnd 2: Work 2 sc in each sc around — 12 sc.

Rnds 3–10: Sc in each sc around — 12 sc. Fill ball before next rnd.

Rnd 11: *Sc in next sc, skip next sc; rep from * 5 times, sl st in next sc to join — 6 sc. Fasten off, leaving a sewing length.

FINISHING

Arrange all of the pieces except the dangling balls (see diagram). With the yarn needle and matching yarn, sew the pieces to the choker.

KNOT STITCH CHAIN

With A, leaving a sewing length at beginning, work 8 knot sts. Fasten off, leaving a sewing length. Sew one end of the chain to the top of one small dangling ball, and the other end to the lower edge of the choker.

SIMPLE CHAIN *(make 2)*

With A, leaving a sewing length at beginning, make a ch approx 3½"/9cm long. Fasten off, leaving a sewing length. Sew one end of one chain to the top of the other small dangling ball, and the other end to the lower edge of the choker. Use the other chain to attach the large dangling ball to the choker in same manner, placing the chain in the center of one ring.

This project was created with

1 skein of Rowan's *Fabulous* Wool Cotton yarn in Chestnut (#966) (A), 50% merino wool, 50% cotton, 1.7oz/50g = 123yd/113m

1 skein each of Lion Brand *Wool-Ease* worsted weight yarn in Chestnut Heather (#179) (B), Forest Green Heather (#180) (C), Loden (#177) (D), Peacock (#70) (E), and White (#100) (F), 80% acrylic, 20% wool, 3oz/20g=197yd/180m

1 ball of Lion Brand *Microspun* sport weight yarn in Mango (#186) (G) and Buttercup (#158) (H), 100% acrylic, 2.5oz/70g = 168yd/154m

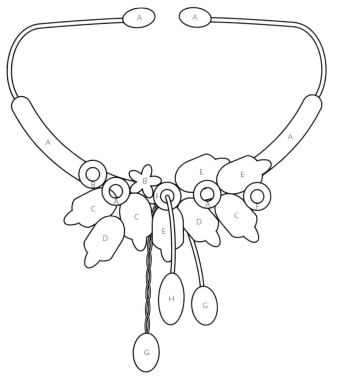

Modular Crochet Pendants

each of these delicate charms makes a smart, distinctive accessory. With bone rings from the craft store and paper yarn in your favorite shade, you can easily crochet all three of these pretty pendants.

To Make the Daisy Charm

FINISHED MEASUREMENTS

2½"/6.5cm x 2½"/6.5cm

PATTERN

Arrange 6 of the bone rings, then work a continuous round of single crochet, filling each ring with stitches while joining rings together in pattern (see diagram).

Rnd 1: Join yarn in Ring 1, ch 1, work 8 sc in interior third of Ring 1, sl st in Ring 2, work 8 sc in interior third of Ring 2, sl st in Ring 3, work 8 sc in interior third of Ring 3, sl st in Ring 4, work 8 sc in interior third of Ring 4, sl st in Ring 5, work 8 sc in interior third of Ring 5, sl st in Ring 6, work 24 sc in Ring 6 to fill, sl st in Ring 5, work 16 sc in remainder of Ring 5, sl st in Ring 4, work 16 sc in remainder of Ring 4, sl st in

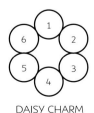

DAISY CHARM

Ring 3, work 16 sc in remainder of Ring 3, sl st in Ring 2, work 16 sc in remainder of Ring 2, sl st in Ring 1, work 16 sc in remainder of Ring 1, working over sts, sl st in Ring 6, sl st in first sc to join. Fasten off. Weave in ends.

FINISHING

Thread the desired length of plastic, hemp or leather cord through the knot cover cap from the base. Make a knot and close the cap over the knot using the needle-nose pliers. Thread the other end of the cord through the other knot cover cap from the base. Make a knot and close the cap over the knot using the needle-nose pliers. Form the prong of the knot cover into a ring, add the jump ring, and clamp the prong shut with the needle-nose pliers. Do the same for the other side, but attach the lobster clasp instead of a jump ring.

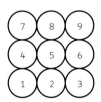

3 x 3 CHARM

To make the 3 x 3 Charm

FINISHED MEASUREMENTS

3½"/9cm x 3½"/9cm

PATTERN

Arrange 9 of the bone rings, then work a continuous round of single crochet, filling each ring with stitches while joining the rings together in the pattern (see diagram).

Rnd 1: Join yarn in Ring 1, ch 1, work 12 sc in lower half of Ring 1, sl st in Ring 2, work

SKILL LEVEL

Intermediate

YOU WILL NEED

Approx 840yd/768m 100% linen fine weight paper yarn

Hook: 2.75mm/C-2

21 ¾"/2cm bone rings

3 pieces of leather, hemp, or plastic cord, each 17"/43cm or desired length

6 double cup knot covers

Needle-nose pliers

3 jump rings, 5mm diameter

3 lobster clasps

Tapestry needle

STITCHES USED

Slip stitch (sl st)

Single crochet (sc)

GAUGE

Exact gauge is not crucial for this pattern.

PATTERN NOTES

The rings in each charm should be completely covered with stitches when finished. Always work sc closely and evenly across each section of rings. In order to provide a number of sts for each section, it has been estimated that the rings will hold 24 sc total, but the exact count is not important. Your materials and gauge may vary. Always work enough sc to fill the section indicated.

work 6 sc in lower left quarter of Ring 9, working over sts, sl st in Ring 6, work 18 sc around remainder of Ring 9, sl st in Ring 8, work 12 sc in upper half of Ring 8, sl st in Ring 7, work 18 sc around remainder of Ring 7, sl st in Ring 4, work 12 sc in left half of Ring, sl st in Ring 1, work 6 sc in remainder of Ring 1, sl st in first sc to join. Fasten off. Weave in ends.

Finish in the same manner as the Daisy Charm.

To make the Triangle Charm

FINISHED MEASUREMENTS

2½"/6.5cm x 2½"/6.5cm

PATTERN

Arrange 6 of the bone rings, then work a continuous round of single crochet, filling each ring with stitches while joining the rings together in the pattern (see diagram).

Rnd 1: Join yarn in Ring 1, ch 1, work 12 sc in upper half of Ring 1, sl st in Ring 2, work 12 sc in upper half of Ring 2, sl st in Ring 3, work 24 sc in Ring 3 to fill, sl st in Ring 2, work 12 sc in lower half of Ring 2, sl st in Ring 1, work 6 sc in lower left quarter of Ring 1, sl st in Ring 4, work 3 sc in upper eighth of Ring 4, sl st in Ring 2, work 3 sc in next eighth of Ring 4, sl st in Ring 5, work 3 sc in upper right eighth of Ring 5, sl st in Ring 2, work 3 sc in next eighth of Ring 5, Ring 3, work 16 sc in remainder of Ring 5, sl st in Ring 3, work 12 sc in next half of Ring 5, working over sts, sl st in Ring 4, work 3 sc in next eighth of Ring 4, sl st in Ring 6, work 24 sc in Ring 6 to fill, sl st in Ring 4, working over sts, work 12 sc around remainder of Ring 4, sl st in Ring 1, work 6 sc in remainder of Ring 1, sl st in first sc to join. Fasten off. Weave in ends.

Finish in the same manner as the Daisy Charm.

These projects were created with

Habu *Shosenshi* Paper (A-60) in eggplant (#116), 100% linen, 3½oz/100g = 1094yds/1000m.

12 sc in lower half of Ring 2, sl st in Ring 3, work 24 sc in Ring 3, sl st in Ring 2, work 12 sc in upper half of Ring 2, sl st in Ring 1, work 6 sc in upper right quarter of Ring 1, sl st in Ring 4, work 6 sc in lower right quarter of Ring 4, sl st in Ring 5, work 6 sc in lower left quarter of Ring 5, working over sts, sl st in Ring 2, work 6 sc in lower right quarter of Ring 5, sl st in Ring 6, work 6 sc in lower left

TRIANGLE CHARM

quarter of Ring 6, working over sts, sl st in Ring 3, work 18 sc around remainder of Ring 6, sl st in Ring 5, work 12 sc in upper half of Ring 5, sl st in Ring 4, work 6 sc in upper right quarter of Ring 4, sl st in Ring 7, work 6 sc in lower right quarter of Ring 7, sl st in Ring 8, work 6 sc in lower left quarter of Ring 8, working over sts, sl st in Ring 8, work 6 sc in lower right quarter of Ring 8, sl st in Ring 9,

Four Pendant Cords

DESIGNER · **Vashti Braha**

do you have
a special
charm or bead
you're eager to show off?
Make one of these
pendant cords—or
crochet all four—and
you can display your
favorite pieces in style.

SKILL LEVEL

Intermediate

FINISHED MEASUREMENTS

Approx 18"/45.5cm long

YOU WILL NEED

1 50g ball of size 20 cotton crochet thread in myrtle green

Hook: size 1mm/12 or size needed to obtain gauge

Jewelry clasps

Fine embroidery needle

STITCHES USED

Chain stitch (ch)

Slip stitch (sl st)

Single crochet (sc)

Double crochet (dc)

Bobble: (Yo, insert hook in next st, draw up a ⅛"/3mm loop) twice in same st, yo, draw yarn through 3 loops, yo, draw yarn through 2 loops on hook.

Clones Knot: Draw up loop on hook to ¼"/6mm, (yo, insert hook around body of ¼"/6mm loop, yo, draw up a loop) 5 times, yo, draw through all 11 loops on hook.

GAUGE

Exact gauge is not crucial for this project. 12 sts = 1"/2.5cm.

PATTERN NOTES

Depending on the type of jewelry clasp you use, the clasp may be crocheted on at the beginning and end of the cord, or you may leave a 10"/25.5cm tail at each end for sewing the clasp on after crocheting.

BUNNY PATH CORD

This cord is designed for pendants with a hole on each side. Two cords that are mirror images of each other are made separately and joined to each end of the pendant.

Cord for right pendant hole (when worn)

Leaving a 10"/25.5cm tail, ch 102 (or a multiple of 10 plus 2) to measure 9½"/24cm.

Row 1: Working in bottom loop of each ch, sc in 2nd ch from hook, sc in each ch across, turn — 101 sc.

Row 2: Ch 1, sc in each of first 5 sc, ★ch 3, skip next 2 sc, bobble in next sc, ch 3, skip next 2 sc★★, sc in each of next 5 sc; rep from ★ across, ending last rep at ★★, sc in last sc, turn — 10 bobbles made.

Row 3: Ch 1, sc in first sc, ★3 sc in next ch-3 loop, sc in next bobble, 3 sc in next ch-3 loop, sc in each of next 5 sc; rep from ★ across. Do not fasten off.

To attach to pendant: Ch 18 (you may need to add chains to fit thick pendants), skip next 3 row-end sts, sl st in end st of foundation ch, feed loop of ch-18 through pendant hole from front to back; on WS of cord, sl st together 9th ch of ch-18 to row-end st of Row 1, sl st 10th ch of ch-18 to row-end st of Row 2. Fasten off securely and weave in end.

Cord for left pendant hole (when worn)

Work same as for right pendant cord through Row 1.

Row 2: Ch 1, sc in each of first sc, ★ch 3, skip next 2 sc, bobble in next sc, ch 3, skip next 2 sc, sc in each of next 5 sc; rep from ★ across, ch 18 and attach pendant same as for Right Pendant Cord but do not fasten off.

Row 3: Working across Row 2, sc in each of first 5 sc, ★3 sc in next ch-3 loop, sc in next bobble, 3 sc in next ch-3 loop★★, sc in each of next 5 sc; rep from ★ across, ending last rep at ★★, sc in last sc. Fasten off. Weave in end.

Attach clasp by using the 10"/25.5cm tails and fine embroidery needle.

OFFSET SCALLOPS CORD

Depending on the clasp you use, you can thread the beginning ch-6 through the clasp to attach it before joining the ch-6 into a ring; then do the same with the last ch-6 of the cord.

Leaving a 10"/25.5cm tail, ch 6, sc in first ch to form a ring.

Row 1: Ch 1, (5 sc, ch 6, sc) in ring, turn.

Row 2: Ch 1, (5 sc, ch 6, sc) in next ch-6 loop, turn.

Rep Row 2 until cord measures 18"/45.5cm. Fasten off, leaving a 10"/25.5cm tail. Suspend the pendant on the cord and attach the clasp. Weave in ends.

OFFSET DIAMONDS CORD

Depending on the clasp you use, you can thread the beginning ch-8 through the clasp to attach it before joining the ch-8 into a ring. Then do the same with the last ch-6 of the cord after suspending the pendant.

Leaving a 10"/25.5cm tail, ch 8, sl st in first ch to form a ring.

Row 1: Ch 3, (5 dc, ch 6, sc) in ring, turn.

Row 2: Ch 3, (5 dc, ch 6, sc) in next ch-6 loop, turn.

Rep Row 2 until cord measures 18"/45.5cm. Fasten off, leaving a 10"/25.5cm tail. Suspend the pendant on the cord and attach the clasp. Weave in ends.

These projects were created with

1 ball of Coats *Opera* Crochet Thread, size
20, in myrtle green (#518), 100% cotton,
1.75oz/50g = 443y/405m.

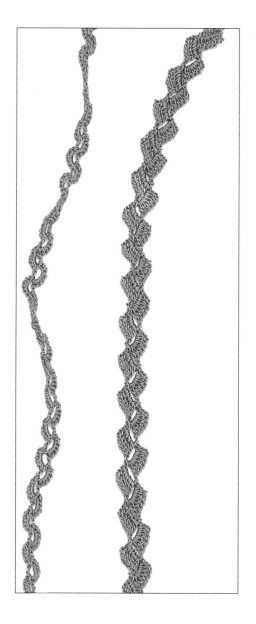

Knot Stitch Necklace

DESIGNER · **ELIZABETA NEDELJKOVICH-MARTONOSI**

this versatile necklace offers plenty of options. To give it a laid-back look, use natural hemp and earthy wooden accents.

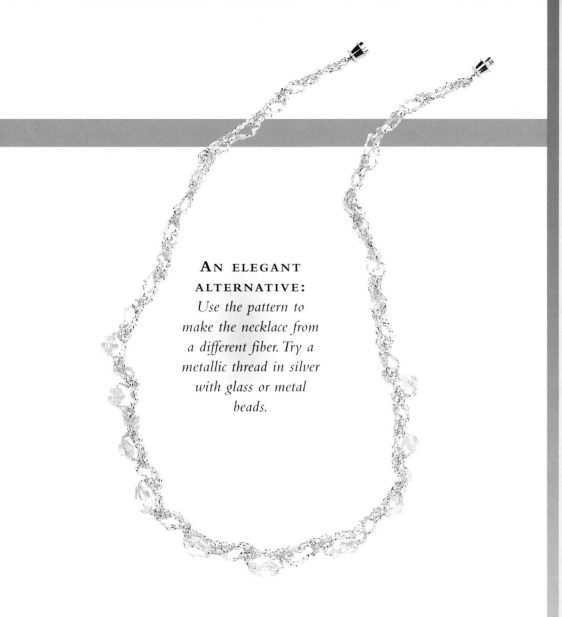

**AN ELEGANT
ALTERNATIVE:**
*Use the pattern to
make the necklace from
a different fiber. Try a
metallic thread in silver
with glass or metal
beads.*

SKILL LEVEL:
Easy

FINISHED MEASUREMENTS
Approx 22"/53.5cm

YOU WILL NEED
Approx 3½yd/3.2m 100% sport weight natural hemp

Hook: size 3.75mm/F-5

18 oblong dark wooden beads, 10 x 6 mm

2 round dark wooden beads, 10 mm

3 round dark wooden beads, 12mm

Sewing needle with a large eye

Bar and ring toggle clasp

STITCHES USED
Knot stitch (knot st): Draw up a loop to ½"/1.3cm, yo, draw yarn through long loop on hook (ch made), insert hook in single strand (bottom part) of long loop just made, yo, draw yarn through loop, yo, draw through 2 loops on hook (sc made to complete knot st).

Beaded Knot stitch (beaded knot st): Draw up a loop to ½"/1.3cm, draw bead up close to work, yo, draw yarn through long loop on hook (ch made), insert hook in single strand (bottom part) of long loop just made, yo, draw yarn through loop, yo, draw through 2 loops on hook (sc made to complete knot st).

GAUGE
Exact gauge is not crucial for this pattern.

STRINGING BEADS

Before starting, string the wooden beads onto the hemp in the following order: Nine 10 x 6mm, one 10mm, three 12mm, one 10 mm, and the the remaining nine 10 x 6mm beads. Use the needle to thread the yarn through the beads. Leave about 4"/10 cm of loose yarn before the place where you start.

TO MAKE THE NECKLACE

Leaving a 4"/10cm sewing length, make a slip knot on yarn, work 2 knot sts without beads, work 23 beaded knot sts, work 2 knot sts without beads. Fasten off, leaving a 4"/10 cm sewing length. Use the sewing lengths to attach the parts of the clasp.

This project was made with

1 ball of *Elements* hemp in taupe/beige (#1833), 3½oz/100g = 100yd/91.4m.

Delicate Silver Choker

Pair this enchanting silver band with your favorite dress, whether it's a romantic print or classic black velvet. Crocheted from sparkling embroidery floss, the choker is lighter than air, yet very versatile.

PATTERN

Ch 85.

Row 1 (WS): Sc in 2nd ch from hook, sc in each of next 2 ch, ★ch 6, skip next 6 ch, sc in each of next 3 ch; rep from ★ across, turn — 9 ch-6 loops.

Work now progresses in rnds.

Rnd 2: ★13 sc in next ch-6 loop, skip next st, sl st in next st★; rep from ★ to ★ across, working across opposite side of foundation ch, rep from ★ to ★ across.

Row 3: ★★Ch 9, skip next 3 sc, dc in next sc, (ch 2, skip next 2 sc, dc in next sc) twice, ★ch 3, skip next 6 sc, dc in next sc, (ch 2, skip next 2 sc, dc in next sc) twice; rep from ★ across to last loop of choker, ch 9, skip next 3 sc, sl st in end sc of Row 1; rep from ★★ once, ending with sl st in end of first sc in Row 1.

Row 4: Ch 1, ★★9 sc in next ch-9 loop, sc in next dc, (2 sc in next ch-2 space, sc in next dc) twice, ★3 sc in next ch-3 loop, sc in next dc, (2 sc in next ch-2 space, sc in next dc) twice; rep from ★ across to last loop of choker, 9 sc in next ch-9 loop; rep from ★★ once, ch 9 for button loop, sl st in first sc to join. Fasten off. Weave in ends.

FINISHING

Press the choker using a doubled pressing cloth and a warm iron. Do not touch the metallic yarn directly with the iron. The choker may be stretched or shortened to fit during this process. Sew the silver button to the end of the choker opposite the button loop using the gray sewing thread.

This project was created with

4 skeins of Presencia *Mouline Especial* 6-Strand Embroidery Floss in Silver (#3000), 35% metallic polyester, 65% viscose, 8.7yd/8m.

SKILL LEVEL

Intermediate

FINISHED MEASUREMENTS

Approx 1½"/3.8cm x 14½"/37cm

YOU WILL NEED

Approx 35yd/32m 6-strand embroidery floss in silver

Hook: size 2mm/3

Needle with eye large enough to thread the floss

Sewing needle

Sewing thread in gray

1 silver button, ¾"/2cm

STITCHES USED

Chain stitch (ch)

Slip stitch (sl st)

Single crochet (sc)

Double crochet (dc)

GAUGE

Exact gauge is not crucial to this pattern. 7 sc = 1"/2.5cm.

Sunflowers Collar

ertain to make
you smile.

This free-spirited choker

can be made with one

or two sunflowers.

Brown seed beads make

the blossoms glow.

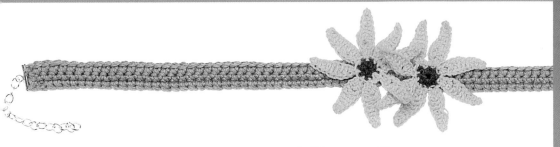

DESIGNER · LINDSAY STREEM

SKILL LEVEL

Intermediate

FINISHED MEASUREMENTS

Sunflowers: Approx 2"/5cm in diameter

Neck band: 12"/30.5cm long (adjustable), excluding chain

YOU WILL NEED

Approx ½yd/.5m per flower of cotton crochet thread, size 10, in brown (A)

Approx 4½yd/4.1m per flower of cotton crochet thread, size 10, in golden yellow (B)

10yd/9m of cotton crochet thread, size 3, in sage green (C)

Hooks: 1.6mm/6 and 2mm/3

Fabric stiffener

Sewing needle

Clear nylon quilting thread

Glass seed beads in brown, size 6

2 triple strand connectors

Needle-nose pliers

2 jump rings, 6mm diameter

2"/5cm of medium-size silver chain

Lobster claw clasp

STITCHES USED

Chain st (ch)

Slip stitch (sl st)

Single crochet (sc)

Half double crochet (hdc)

Double crochet (dc)

Treble crochet (tr)

GAUGE

Sunflower = 2"/5cm in diameter. In neck band pattern, 13 sts = 2"/5cm

SUNFLOWER *(for Version A, make 1; for Version B, make 2)*

With A and the smaller hook, ch 5, sl st in first ch to form ring.

Rnd 1 (RS): Ch 2, 7 hdc in ring, sl st in 2nd ch of beginning ch-2 to join – 8 hdc. Fasten off.

Rnd 2: With RS facing, join B in any hdc, ch 1, sc in first st, *ch 10, sc in second ch from hook, sc in next ch, hdc in each of next 2 ch, dc in each of next 2 ch, tr in next ch, dc in next ch, hdc in next ch**, sc in next hdc; rep from * around, ending last rep at **, sl st in first sc to join – 8 petals. Fasten off. Weave in ends.

NECK BAND

With the larger hook and C, ch 80.

Row 1: Sc in 2nd ch from hook, sc in each ch across being careful not to twist ch, turn — 79 sc.

Row 2–3: Ch 1, sc in each sc across, turn — 79 sc. Fasten off. Weave in ends.

FINISHING

Following the instructions on page 124, lightly stiffen each flower with the fabric stiffener. Shape the petals of each flower as they dry.

VERSION A

After the flower is completely dry, use the sewing needle and quilting thread to sew the beads to the center of the sunflower. Then center the sunflower on the neckband and use the sewing needle and quilting thread to sew it to the neckband.

VERSION B

Position the two sunflowers on the center of the neckband, so that they overlap, with the centers of the flowers approximately 1"/2.5cm apart. Then use the sewing needle and quilting thread to sew the sunflowers to the neckband.

BOTH VERSIONS

Use the quilting thread and the sewing needle to sew the connectors to each end of the choker on the back. Use the needle-nose pliers to open one of the jump rings, and slip the ring through the end link in the piece of chain. Then slip the jump ring with the chain through the end loop of the connector on the left end of the choker, and close the jump ring with the needle-nose pliers.

Use the needle-nose pliers to open the other jump ring, add the lobster clasp to the ring, then slip the ring with the clasp on it through the end loop of the connector on the right end of the choker. Use the needle-nose pliers to close the ring.

This project was created with

1 ball of Aunt Lydia's *Classic* Crochet Cotton Thread, size 10, in Fudge Brown (#0131) (A), 100% mercerized cotton, 350yd/320m

1 ball of J&P Coats *Royale* Classic Crochet Thread, size 10, in Golden Yellow (#432) (B), 100% mercerized cotton, 350yd/320m

1 ball of Aunt Lydia's *Fashion* Crochet Thread, size 3, in Sage (#625) (C), 100% mercerized cotton, 150yd/137m.

Leafy Garden Necklace

S parkling sprays of bicone beads make this piece special. The bead embellishments are easy to add—simply sew them to the necklace with a needle and matching thread.

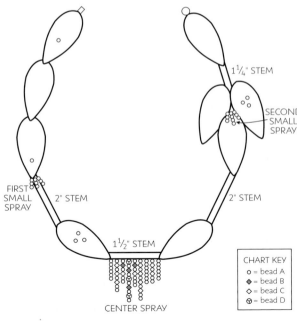

1¼" STEM

SECOND SMALL SPRAY

FIRST SMALL SPRAY

2" STEM

2" STEM

1½" STEM

CENTER SPRAY

CHART KEY
○ = bead A
◆ = bead B
◇ = bead C
⊕ = bead D

LEAF (make 9)

Leaving a 6"/15cm tail, ch 10.

Row 1: Sl st in 2nd ch from hook, sc in each of next 2 ch, hdc in each of next 2 ch, dc in each of next 2 ch, tr in next ch, 8 tr in last ch, working across opposite side of foundation ch, tr in next ch, dc in each of next 2 ch, hdc in each of next 2 ch, sc in each of next 2 ch, sl st in next ch at base of sl st at beg. Fasten off, leaving a 6"/15cm tail.

STEM (make two 2"/5cm long, one 1½"/4cm long, and one 1¼"/3cm long)

Leaving a 6"/15cm tail, ch 3, sl st into first ch to form a ring.

Rnd 1: Ch 1, sc in front loop only of each ch around, do not join. Work in a spiral.

Rnd 2: Sc in front loop of each sc around.

Rep Rnd 2 until stem measures desired length, sl st in next sc to join. Fasten off, leaving a 6"/15cm tail.

ASSEMBLY

Using the embroidery needle and the beginning and ending tails, sew the leaves and stems together (see diagram). Using the flexible beading needle and the yarn tails, attach the pieces of the clasp to each end of the necklace. Weave in the ends, then apply jeweler's glue to the cut ends.

BEADING

Using the size 10 beading needle and the nylon beading thread, sew 8 A beads to the leaves to represent dew. Knot the beading thread and weave in the ends.

SMALL BEAD SPRAY (make 2)

With the size 10 beading needle, attach the beading thread to the stem. ★Slide 3 A beads for the first bead strand onto the beading needle and slide the beads up close to the stem, skip the bottom bead, insert the beading needle up through the previous bead and through the remaining beads in the strand, then insert it into the stem fabric; rep from ★ for each bead strand across. Weave in the ends. Apply jeweler's glue to cut ends.

Work a second spray in the same manner.

CENTER BEAD SPRAY

Work the same as the first small spray.

This project was created with

1 ball of Cascade Yarns *Fixation* yarn in green variegated (#9385), 98.3% cotton/1.7% elastic, 1oz/50g = 100yd/92m.

SKILL LEVEL

Intermediate

FINISHED MEASUREMENTS

Approx 16"/40.5cm long (excluding clasp)

YOU WILL NEED

35yd/32m cotton/elastic blend yarn (#3 Light) in variegated greens

Hook: size 2.25mm/B-1

Embroidery needle

Flexible beading needle

Gold rose box clasp, 10mm

Jeweler's glue

Size 10 beading needle

1 spool of nylon B weight beading thread

76 clear, round faceted beads, 3mm (A)

4 purple bicone beads, 4mm (B)

11 pink bicone beads, 4mm (C)

3 yellow faceted coin beads, 6mm (D)

STITCHES USED

Chain stitch (ch)

Slip stitch (sl st)

Single crochet (sc)

Half double crochet (hdc)

Double crochet (dc)

Treble crochet (tr)

GAUGE

Exact gauge is not crucial to this project.
Leaf = 1 x 2"/2.5 x 5cm.

Lavender Lariat

a n easy-to-crochet cord is paired with a tassel of playful beads for a fresh take on the traditional lariat. Use the loop to adjust the length of the piece.

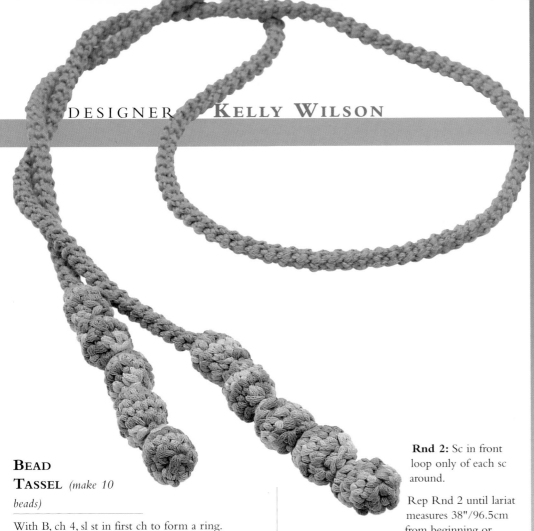

DESIGNER KELLY WILSON

SKILL LEVEL

Easy

FINISHED MEASUREMENTS

Length: 45½"/115.5cm long

Note: Necklace will be folded in half when worn.

YOU WILL NEED

30yd/27.5m corn fiber yarn in lavender (A)

30yd/27.5m corn fiber variegated yarn in yellow, blue, green, and lavender (B)

Hook: size 2.75mm/C-2

Tapestry needle

Jeweler's glue

STITCHES USED

Chain stitch (ch)

Slip stitch (sl st)

Single crochet (sc)

Sc2tog: (Insert hook in next st, yo, draw yarn through st) twice, yo, draw yarn through 3 loops on hook.

GAUGE

Exact gauge is not crucial to this project. Ball = approx ⅝ x ¾"/1.6 x 2cm. In lariat pattern, 5 rows sc = 1"/2.5cm.

BEAD

TASSEL *(make 10 beads)*

With B, ch 4, sl st in first ch to form a ring.

Rnd 1: Ch 1, 6 sc in ring, sl st into first sc to join — 6 sc.

Rnd 2: Ch 1, sc in first sc, ★2 sc in next sc, sc in next sc; rep from ★ around, ending with 2 sc in last sc, sl st into first sc to join — 9 sc.

Rnd 3: Ch 1, sc in each sc around, sl st in first sc to join — 9 sc.

Rnd 4: Ch 1, sc in first sc, ★sc2tog in next 2 sts, sc in next sc; rep from ★ around, ending with sc2tog in last 2 sts, sl st into first sc to join — 6 sc. Fasten off. Use crochet hook to weave in ends (a tapestry needle will split the yarn). Apply jeweler's glue to cut ends.

LARIAT

With A, leaving a 12"/30.5cm tail, ch 3, sl st in first ch to form a ring.

Rnd 1: Ch 1, 4 sc in ring, do not join. Work in a spiral.

Rnd 2: Sc in front loop only of each sc around.

Rep Rnd 2 until lariat measures 38"/96.5cm from beginning or 7"/18cm less than desired length, sl st in next sc to join. Fasten off, leaving a 12"/30.5cm tail.

FINISHING

Using the tapestry needle and the 12"/30.5cm tail at one end of the lariat, slide on 5 beads, inserting the needle through each bead at the center hole at the beginning and ending rounds. Weave the end into the last bead. Repeat this step for the opposite end of the lariat. Apply jeweler's glue to the cut ends.

To wear the necklace, fold the cord in half and place it around your neck. Pull the beaded ends through the loop and adjust it with the beads slightly off-center.

This project was created with

1 ball each of South West Trading Company *aMAIZing* in Purple Gumdrop (#156) and Child's Play (#164), 100% corn fiber, 1.75oz/50g = 143yd/130m.

Rowanberry Pendant

the Clones **t**knot, a classic Irish crochet stitch, is used to produce this pretty pendant. Black velvet ribbon adds a touch of timeless sophistication.

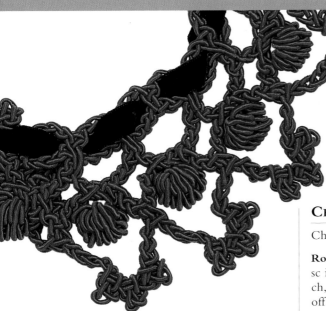

PATTERN NOTES

Wash your hands often to keep the cotton cord looking fresh. To hand-block your stitches, spritz them with water and tug on them evenly in all directions to open up ch-spaces and position the picots so that they'll lie flat. If the picots won't lie flat, then they were probably twisted as they were crocheted. Let the necklace dry completely. When cotton cord is worked at a tight gauge like this one, it tends to retain the shape to which it is blocked.

CENTER PANEL

Ch 28.

Rnd 1 (WS): Working bottom loops of ch sts, sc in 2nd ch from hook, *ch 6, skip next 4 ch, sc in next ch*; rep from * to * once, ch 6, skip next 5 ch, sc in next ch, rep from * to * once, ch 6, skip next 4 ch, (sc, dc, 3 picots, ch 1, sc) in last ch, working across opposite side of foundation ch, **ch 3, skip next 4 ch, work long sc in next sc on other side of foundation ch**; rep from ** to ** once, ch 3, skip next 2 ch, sc in next ch, ch 3, skip next 2 ch, long sc in next sc, rep from ** to ** once, ch 3, (sc, ch 1, 3 picots, dc) in next ch, sl st in first sc to join.

Work now progresses in rows.

Row 2: Ch 3, *sc in 3rd ch of next ch-6 loop, work clones knot, sl st in next ch**, ch 6; rep from * 3 times, rep from * to ** once, ch 2, sc in top of dc, turn.

Row 3: *Ch 4, 3 picots, ch 4**, sc in 3rd ch of next ch-6 loop; rep from * 3 times, rep from * to ** once, sl st in 2nd ch of next ch-3 loop. Fasten off.

CHAIN LINKS (make 2)

Ch 14.

Row 1 (RS): Working bottom loops of ch sts, sc in 2nd ch from hook, *ch 2, skip next 2 ch, sc in next ch; rep from * 3 times. Fasten off. Weave in ends.

TO MOUNT THE NECKLACE ONTO THE RIBBON

Cut the ribbon to the desired length (it should be long enough to fit around the neck and be tied in a bow). Weave the ribbon through the spaces of the necklace created by the second half of Rnd 1. Weave one end of the ribbon through the spaces in one chain link on one side of the center panel. Repeat on the other side of the center panel. Fold the ribbon end ½"/13mm from the end, wrong sides together, and wrap it tightly with the cord 5 times. Tuck in the ends with a needle or small crochet hook, pull the ends tightly, and trim them. A dot of glue may be added to the ribbon before wrapping it with the cord. Repeat these steps on the other end of ribbon.

This project was created with

1 hank of Judi & Co.'s *Cordé* in Red, 100% rayon with a cotton core, 144yd/132m.

SKILL LEVEL

Intermediate

FINISHED MEASUREMENTS

Center Panel: approx 2¾"/7cm x 6"/15cm

Necklace: 18"/45.5cm (adjustable)

YOU WILL NEED

Approx 16yd/15m medium-weight rayon-wrapped cotton cord

Hook: size 3mm/D-3 or size needed to obtain gauge

30"/76cm of black velvet ribbon, ⅜"/10mm wide

Yarn needle

Clear glue (optional)

STITCHES USED

Chain stitch (ch)

Single crochet (sc)

Double crochet (dc)

Picot: Ch 4, sl st in 4th ch from hook.

Long single crochet: Insert hook in center of sc of row below, draw up a loop to the height of a sc, yo, draw yarn through 2 loops on hook.

Clones Knot: Draw up loop on hook to 1"/2.5cm, (yo, insert hook around body of 1"/2.5cm loop, yo, draw up a loop) 5 times, yo, draw through all 11 loops on hook.

GAUGE

22 ch sts = 4"/10cm. Take time to check your gauge.

Curlicue Necklace

this colorful corkscrew is simple to make using a basic double crochet stitch. Accented with cheerful ribbons, it'll add a dose of color to your day.

PATTERN

Leaving a sewing length, ch 110 (approximately 20"/53.5cm long).

Work 2 dc in 3rd ch from the hook, 3 dc in each ch across. Fasten off leaving a long sewing length. This will form a 17"/43cm long corkscrew.

FINISHING

Using the tapestry needle, work in the tail, stitching the last corkscrew formation into a loop. Do the same with the tail at the beginning. Cut the pink and purple ribbon into two 18"/46cm pieces. Then tie a piece of the pink ribbon and a piece of the purple ribbon together at one end using an overhand knot. With the tapestry needle, thread the knotted ribbon into the base of one end and pull the ribbon until the knot is next to the corkscrew. Do the same on the other side. To wear the necklace, tie the ribbons in a bow at the back of your neck.

This project was created with

1 skein of Artyarn *Regal Silk* in pink and purple variegated (#111), 100% silk, 1¾oz/50g = 163yd/149m.

SKILL LEVEL

Easy

FINISHED MEASUREMENTS

17"/43cm without ribbons

YOU WILL NEED

Approx 163yd/149m 100% silk sport weight yarn

Hook: size 2.75mm/C-2

Tapestry needle

1 yd/.9m of pink double-faced satin ribbon, ⅛"/3mm wide

1 yd/.9m of lavender double faced satin ribbon, ⅛"/3mm wide

STITCHES USED

Chain stitch (ch)

Double crochet (dc)

GAUGE

Exact gauge is not crucial for this pattern. Measuring tops of sts, 6 sts = 1"/2.5cm

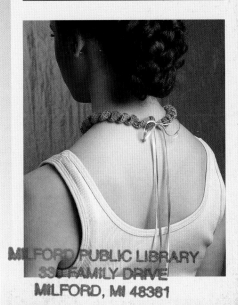

MILFORD PUBLIC LIBRARY
330 FAMILY DRIVE
MILFORD, MI 48381

Adorn the Hand & Wrist

Cuffs . Bangles . Rings

Fiesta Bangles

DESIGNER · GWEN BLAKLEY KINSLER

FINISHED MEASUREMENTS

1"/2.5cm bangle:

Inner lining: 8¼"/21cm x ¾"/2cm

Outer cover: 10½"/26.5cm x 1¼"/3.2cm

1½"/3.8cm bangle:

Inner lining: 8"/20.5cm x 1¼"/3.2cm

Outer cover: 10"/25.5cm x 1¾"/4.5cm

YOU WILL NEED

Approx 33yd/30m each of metallic thread (equivalent to #10 crochet thread) in gold (A), chartreuse (B), and turquoise (C)

Approx 66yd/60m metallic thread (equivalent to #10 crochet thread) in red (D)

Approx 44yd/40m metallic thread (equivalent to #10 crochet thread) in purple (E)

Hook: size 1.5mm/7 or size needed to obtain gauge

Tapestry needle

2 light chartreuse bangle bracelets, each 1"/2.5cm wide

1 light purple bangle bracelet, 1½"/3.8cm wide

a dazzling net of crocheted thread gives the traditional bangle bracelet new life. The design possibilities are boundless —you can dream up your own color schemes, or stick to the examples you see here.

PATTERN NOTES

When joining the lining to the outer cover, adjust the number of rows between sl sts, if necessary. Be sure to work the ch st and sl st tightly when joining the lining to the outer cover. Stretch the ch loops, not the ch or sl st. Stretch the ch-3 loops and adjust the lining when ⅓ of the outer cover is attached to the second side of the lining.

FIRST 1"/2.5CM BRACELET

Inner lining

With A, ch 8 (or enough ch sts to fit the width of the inner circumference).

Row 1: Sc in 2nd ch from the hook, sc in each ch across, turn — 7 sc.

Row 2: Ch 1, sc in each sc across, turn — 7 sc.

Rep Row 2 until lining measures 8¼"/21cm or length to cover the inside circumference of bracelet. With RS tog, working through double thickness, join last row to foundation ch by working sl st in each st across. Fasten off. Weave in ends.

Outer cover

With B, ch 90 (or desired number to fit outer circumference of bracelet snugly), and without twisting ch, sl st in first ch to form a ring.

Rnd 1: ★Ch 3, skip next 2 ch, sl st in next ch; rep from ★ around, ending with ch 1, dc in first ch of beg ch-3 — 30 ch-3 loops.

Rnd 2: ★Ch 3, sl st in second ch of next loop; rep from ★ around, ending with ch 1, dc in top of ending dc of previous rnd — 30 ch-3 loops.

Rep Rnd 2 (5 times). Do not fasten off.

Joining the lining to the outer cover

With WS of outer cover and lining facing, sl st in end of any row of lining, ch 1, sl st in 2nd ch of next ch-3 loop, ★ch 1, skip 2 rows on lining, sl st in next row — end st, ch 1, sl st in 2nd ch of next loop; rep from ★ around, ending with ch 1, sl st below beg ch 1. Fasten off. Weave in ends.

Enclosing the bangle

With RS facing, place lining inside bracelet, stretch cover over bracelet. Join B with a sl st in opposite side of cover in 2nd ch of any ch-2 space on foundation ch, ch 1, sl st in side of lining, ★ch 1, sl st in 2nd ch of next loop, ch 1, skip 2 rows on lining, sl st in next row; rep from ★ around. Fasten off. Weave in ends.

SECOND 1"/2.5CM BRACELET

Work same as the first bracelet, using D for the inner lining and C for the outer cover.

1½"/3.8CM BRACELET

Inner lining

With E, ch 12 (or enough ch to fit width of inner circumference).

Row 1: Sc in 2nd ch from the hook, sc in each ch across, turn — 11 sc.

Row 2: Ch 1, sc in each sc across, turn — 11 sc.

Rep Row 2 until lining measures 8"/20.5cm or length to cover the inside circumference of the bracelet. With RS tog, working through double thickness, join last row to foundation ch by working sl st in each st across. Fasten off. Weave in ends.

Outer cover

With D, ch 90 (or desired number to fit outer circumference of bracelet snugly), and without twisting ch, sl st in first ch to form a ring.

Rnd 1: ★Ch 3, skip next 2 ch, sl st in next ch; rep from ★ around, ending with ch 1, dc in first ch of beg ch-3 — 30 ch-3 loops.

Rnd 2: ★Ch 3, sl st in second ch of next loop; rep from ★ around, ending with ch 1, dc in top of ending dc of previous rnd — 30 ch-3 loops.

Rep Rnd 2 (14 times). Do not fasten off.

With D, join outer cover to lining same as for 1" bangle bracelet.

This project was created with

3 spools of Kreinik's *Fine* (#8) Braid in Dark Japan Gold (#321J) (A), Chartreuse (#015) (B), and Turquoise (#029) (C), 11yd/10m

6 spools of Kreinik's *Fine* (#8) Braid in Azalea (#421) (D) , 11yd/10m

4 spools of Kreinik's *Fine* (#8) Braid in Purple High Lustre (#012HL) (E), 11yd/10m.

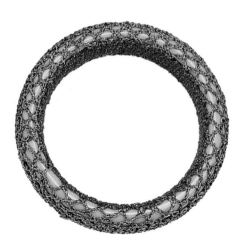

Beaded Tapestry Cuff

S tudded with seed beads, this multi-colored cuff has the look and feel of an old-fashioned tapestry.

DESIGNER · CAROL VENTURA

PATTERN NOTES

Before you start to crochet, thread a beading needle onto both types of thread. Then load the size 8 beads onto thread A and the size 6 beads onto thread B. To create the motif, two bead-strung threads (each with a different color and size of bead) are crocheted at the same time. One thread is carried while the other is crocheted, creating a pattern on both sides of the cloth as the colors are switched. To change colors, work the first color until two loops remain on the hook, yarn over with the second color, draw the yarn through the two loops on the hook, and continue to work with the second color.

BRACELET

Rnd 1: With thread A, make a slip knot leaving a 6"/15cm tail, then ch 70. Inc or dec in multiples of 7 ch to make a larger or smaller bracelet. Join the ends together to form a circle, then work 1 bsc in first ch, carry the tail for 2"/5cm and bsc in each ch around, then drop the tail and begin to carry thread B, leaving a 6"/15 cm tail, working over strand of B, bsc in each remaining st around, do not join — 70 bsc (Row 1 of chart complete). Work in a spiral, marking last st of rnd and moving marker up as work progresses. Work in bsc following chart or work from instructions that follow. To work from chart, work all rnds from right to left, work from A to B once, rep from A to B around.

Rnds 2–8: ★With A, working over strand of B, work 2 bsc, complete last st with B, drop A; with B, working over strand of A, work 5 bsc, complete last st with A, drop B; rep from ★ around — 70 bsc.

Rnds 9–10: With A, working over strand of B, bsc in each st around — 70 bsc. At end of last rnd, with A, sl st in next st to join. Cut B, flush. Fasten off A, leaving 6"/15cm tail. Weave in end.

BOTTOM EDGING

Rnd 1: Turn the bracelet over, then pull on the A and B tails to cinch the diameter of the bracelet to match the other side. Working across opposite side of foundation ch, leaving a 12"/30cm tail, join A in any ch, with A, ch 1, bsc in same ch, working over tail of A, bsc in each ch around, sl st in first bsc to join. Fasten off A, leaving 6"/15cm tail. Weave in ends.

FINISHING

Block the bracelet with a steam iron from the cloth side, making sure that the beads do not get too hot.

This project was created with

⅕ of a ball of DMC *Senso* in Terra Cotta (#1005) (A), 100% cotton, 1.8oz/50g = 150yd/135m

⅒ of a ball of DMC *Senso* in Dusty Rose (#1008) (B), 100% cotton, 1.8 oz/50g = 150yd/135m.

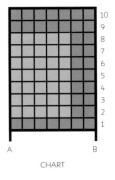

CHART

■ = bsc in A
■ = bsc in B

SKILL LEVEL

Intermediate

FINISHED MEASUREMENTS

Circumference: 8½"/21.5cm

Height: 1½"/4cm

YOU WILL NEED

30yd/27m of size 3 crochet cotton in terra cotta (A)

15yd/14m of size 3 crochet cotton in dusty rose (B)

Crochet hook: size 2.35mm/1

2 heavy beading needles

420 size 8 seed beads in black

350 size 6 beads in clear lilac

Stitch marker

STITCHES USED

Chain stitch (ch)

Slip stitch (sl st)

Single crochet (sc)

Bead single crochet (bsc): Insert hook in next sts, slide bead up to work, yo, draw yarn through st, yo, draw yarn through 2 loops on hook (Note: bead will appear on back of st).

GAUGE

8 sts and 8 rows sc = 1"/2.5cm

Space Age Bracelet

made from clear faceted beads and monofilament fishing line, this futuristic wristlet is sure to become a conversation piece. Crochet never looked so cool.

DESIGNER · PAULA GRON

PATTERN NOTES

You can choose from two different methods for making this bracelet. With the sew-on method, the beads are sewn on after completing the crocheted bracelet. The crocheted-in method gives you the option of placing the beads around each ring while crocheting the bracelet.

If the crocheted-in method is used, the chain part of the stitch will face in, with the beads on the outside of each ring. If the sew-on option is used, sc as per instructions with the chain part of the stitches facing outward. This is the area where you'll sew the beads on.

The monofilament line causes the rings to be springy. When the line is not flexed, the rings overlap. Be sure to account for this stretch when adding or subtracting rings to fit your wrist.

SEW-ON OPTION

Join monofilament in one ring, ★work 11 sc in ring to cover half of ring, working over same ring and next ring, sc in both rings★; rep from ★ to ★ 8 times, work 22 sc in last ring, thus joining 10 rings, working across opposite side of rings, rep from ★ to ★ 9 times, work 11 sc in first ring, without twisting bracelet, sc over first and last ring to join rings, sl st in first sc on first ring to join. Fasten off, leaving 36"/91.5cm length of monofilament. Using tapestry needle, string approx 100 beads on monofilament, working in tops of sts, sew approx 5 beads along each side of each ring. Using tapestry needle, string approx 15 beads on a separate 36"/91.5cm length of monofilament, sew 15 large loops with one bead on each, randomly placed around entire bracelet. Fasten off. Weave in ends.

CROCHETED-IN OPTION

Join monofilament in one ring, ★(sc, bsc) 5 times in ring, sc in ring (should cover half of ring)★★, working over same ring and next ring, sc in both rings★; rep from ★ to ★ 8 times, rep from ★ to ★★ in last ring, thus joining 10 rings (one side complete), working across opposite side of rings, rep from ★ to ★ 9 times, rep from ★ to ★★ in first ring, without twisting bracelet, sc over first and last ring to join rings, sl st in first sc on first ring to join. Fasten off, leaving 36"/91.5cm length of monofilament. Using tapestry needle, string approx 15 beads on length of monofilament, sew 15 large loops with one bead on each, randomly placed around entire bracelet. Fasten off. Weave in ends.

This project was created with

1 spool of Shakespeare *Omniflex* 30 lb. test monofilment fishing line (.023 diameter).

SKILL LEVEL

Easy

FINISHED MEASUREMENTS

Approx 9"/23cm in circumference

YOU WILL NEED

19yd/18m 30 lb. test monofilament fishing line

Hook: size 1.4 mm/8

Approx 115 clear, faceted round beads, 6mm

10 cabone rings, 1"/25mm

Tapestry needle

GAUGE

Gauge is not crucial for this pattern.

STITCHES USED

Single crochet (sc)

Slip stitch (sl st)

Beaded single crochet (bsc) (optional): Insert hook in next st, slide bead up to work, yo, draw yarn through st, yo, draw yarn through 2 loops on hook (Note: bead will appear on back of st).

Chunky Bangles

Covered in crocheted cable cording, these bold, inventive bangles are perfect for any occasion. Dye them any bright shade you like, or go with classic white.

DESIGNER · PAULA GRON

PATTERN

Ch 25 (or desired length to fit loosely over hand), without twisting ch, insert hook through the crossed over loop, sl st to join into a ring.

Rnd 2: Ch 1, working from inside the ring, *working in back loops of sts, sc in each ch around, sl st in back loop of beginning ch-1 to join.

Rnd 3: Ch 1, working from inside, underneath and up, ch 1, *working in front loops of sts, sc in each sc around, sl st in front loop of beginning ch-1 to join. Fasten off. Weave in ends.

FINISHING

You'll need to dye the bangle before the felt lining is applied. Pre-treat the bangle by thoroughly wetting it in warm water. Dissolve ½ of the package of dye in 1c/8oz of hot water, then add ¼c/2oz of salt. Fill a sink or bucket with 1 gal/4L of hot water and add the dye mixture. Soak the wet bangle for up to 30 minutes, depending on the desired intensity of color. Rinse it in warm water, then gradually in cooler water until the water runs clear. Dry the bangle thoroughly before adding the felt lining.

Cut a strip of felt to fit the inner circumference of the bracelet. With the sewing needle and the transparent thread, sew the strip of felt along the inside of the bangle, catching at the same edges of the rope consistently all the way around.

This project was created with

Wright's Cable Cording in white, 100% Polyester, 7/32"/5.5mm.

SKILL LEVEL

Easy

FINISHED MEASUREMENTS

Inner circumference: 8"/20.5cm

Outer circumference: 14"/35.5cm

One size fits most.

YOU WILL NEED

8.5yd/8m bulky weight cable cording (7/32"/5.5mm diameter)

Hook: size 5.5mm/I-9

Stitch marker

Fabric dye in desired color (optional)

Felt square in desired color, 9"/23cm x 12"/30cm

Sewing needle

Transparent thread

GAUGE

8 sts = 4"/10cm

STITCHES USED

Chain stitch (ch)

Single crochet (sc)

Slip stitch (sl st)

PATTERN NOTES

When working the single crochet, work from the inside of the piece. To avoid bulkiness with a big knot at the beginning, use the cord crossed over instead of a slip knot. White cord can be dyed with a fabric dye after finishing, but before sewing in the lining felt.

Floral Rings

t his clever accessory is easy to assemble using a silver band and a headpin. Crochet a garden of gorgeous blossoms and make a ring for every finger!

FLOWER

Ch 2.

Rnd 1: Work 6 sc in 2nd ch from hook, sl st in first sc to join — 6 sc.

Rnd 2: Ch 4, sl st in same sc, ch 4, (sl st, ch 4) twice in each sc around, sl st if first sl st to join.

Fasten off. Weave in ends.

ATTACHING THE FLOWER TO THE RING

Use the hammer and the centerpunch or nail to mark a position for a hole in the center of the silver band. Wearing the safety glasses, carefully drill a hole in the band. If the drill bit skids, make the centerpunch mark a little bigger. Thread the headpin through the hole, coming up from the back, then push the headpin through the hole in the band. The hole in the band should be small enough so that the end of the headpin cannot slip through.

SECURING THE FLOWER TO THE BAND

Put the center of the flower over the headpin. Using the round-nose pliers, bend the headpin into a loop, trapping the flower against the band. Bend the last ¼"/6mm of the headpin into a 90 degree angle. Then tuck it back into the center of the flower and wrap it around the base of the headpin.

These projects were created with

1 skein each of DMC 6-strand embroidery floss in blue (#3843), yellow (#445), orange (#742), and purple (#340), 8.7yd/8m.

SKILL LEVEL

Easy

FINISHED MEASUREMENTS

Flower diameter: ½"/13mm

YOU WILL NEED

1 skein of 6-strand cotton embroidery floss in a bright color of your choice

Hook: size 2mm/3

Sterling silver band, 4mm diameter

Centerpunch or nail

Small hammer

Small-chuck drill press, flex shaft, or hand-held rotary tool

#68 drill bit, or size to match diameter of head pin

Safety glasses

Headpin, 2"/5cm long

Round-nose pliers

STITCHES USED

Chain stitch (ch)

Slip stitch (sl st)

Single crochet (sc)

GAUGE

Flower = ½"/13mm in diameter

Trellis Cuff

made from two separate pieces joined by a simple single crochet edging, this shimmering cuff will add opulence to any outfit.

SKILL LEVEL

Intermediate

FINISHED MEASUREMENTS

2"/5cm x 6¼"/16cm

YOU WILL NEED

Approx 11yd/10m bedspread weight cotton crochet thread in white (A)

Approx 11yd/10m bedspread weight cotton crochet thread in dark beige (B)

Approx 23yd/20.7m metallic embroidery thread in silver (C)

Approx 23yd/20.7m metallic embroidery thread in gold (D)

Hook: 1.4mm/8 or hook that will fit the cotton thread you have

Pearl bead or button, ⅜"/1cm

Darning needle or sharp-pointed needle with eye to fit thread

STITCHES USED

Chain stitch (ch)

Slip stitch (sl st)

Single crochet (sc)

Double crochet (dc)

Treble crochet (tr)

Sc2tog: (Insert hook in next st, yo, draw yarn through st) twice, yo, draw yarn through 3 loops on hook.

GAUGE

Each cotton flower = 1"/2.5cm in diameter. Each metallic flower = ¾"/2cm in diameter. 8 rows and 3 ch-5 loops = 2"/5cm in Trellis pattern. You can also use different hook sizes for the different parts of the cuff, depending on the threads you have.

PATTERN NOTES

The cuff is worked in two pieces that are crocheted together with a sc edging. The first piece consists of two columns of cotton flowers, which have a layer of tiny silver and gold flowers added to them. The second piece consists of the gold and silver trellis that goes behind the cotton flowers. Do not turn your work unless stated. Be careful when attaching the flowers. Make sure that they all face the same way. Work in both loops of stitches except in Rnd 2 of cotton flowers.

FLOWER PANEL

Work 12 flowers, in 2 columns, joining each to previous flower(s) while completing last rnd (see diagram).

FIRST COLUMN OF COTTON FLOWERS

Flower 1

With A, create a foundation loop: With the end of the thread in one hand, wrap the thread around your index finger and hold the thread where it closes into a circle. Insert the hook into the circle. Yo and pull the thread through the circle. If your loop becomes bigger as you work through the wrap, simply tighten it by pulling on the end of the thread.

Rnd 1: Ch 1, work 6 sc into loop. Tighten foundation loop and sl st in first sc to join.

Rnd 2: Ch 1, working in back loops only, (sc, ch 3, 2 tr, ch 3) in each sc around, sl st in first sc to join — 6 petals. Fasten off. Tighten foundation loop and weave in ends.

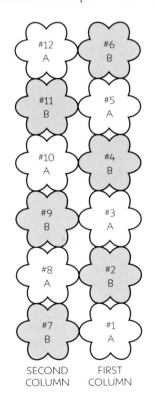

SECOND COLUMN — FIRST COLUMN

Flower 2

With B, work same as Flower 1 up to last 2 petals of Rnd 2, work ★(sc, ch 3 and tr) in next sc, drop loop on hook, insert hook in corresponding stitch on previous flower, pick up dropped loop and draw through st, work (tr, ch 3) in same sc on current flower; rep from ★ in last sc, sl st in first sc to join. Fasten off. Tighten the foundation loop and weave in the ends.

Flowers 3 to 6

Work same as Flower 2, alternating the use of A and B and joining to 2 petals on opposite side of previous flower to form a strip.

At this point, check to make sure that the length of the cuff is right for your wrist. To make the cuff longer, add a flower. To make it tighter, remove a flower.

SECOND COLUMN OF COTTON FLOWERS

As you work through this second column, you will attach it to the first column and to each new flower.

Flower 7

With B, work same as Flower 1 up to last petal of Rnd 2, (sc, ch 3 and tr) in next sc, drop loop on hook, insert hook in corresponding stitch on side of Flower 1 on First Column, pick up dropped loop and draw through st, work (tr, ch 3) in same sc on current flower, sl st in first sc to join. Fasten off. Tighten the foundation loop and weave in the ends.

Flower 8

With A, work same as Flower 1 up to last 3 petals of Rnd 2, ★(sc, ch 3 and tr) in next sc, drop loop on hook, insert hook in corresponding stitch on Flower 2 on First Column, pick up dropped loop and draw through st, work (tr, ch 3) in same sc on current flower; rep from ★ joining to next 2 petals of previous flower on same column, sl st in first sc to join. Fasten off. Tighten the foundation loop and weave in the ends.

Flowers 9 to 12

Work in the same manner as Flower 8, alternating the use of B and A. If you have adjusted for size, make sure the two columns have the same number of flowers and that colors alternate on both sides of cuff.

TINY FLOWERS

Rnd 1: With RS facing, join C in remaining loop of any sc in Rnd 1 of Flower 1, ch 1, working over end of thread so that finishing is easier, (sc, 5 dc) in each st around, sl st in first sc to join. Fasten off. Weave in ends.

Work one metallic flower, same as first metallic flower, in each cotton flower, using C on white (A) flowers and D on dark beige (B) flowers (see diagram).

TRELLIS

With one strand each of C and D held together as one, ch 26.

Row 1 (RS): Dc in 14th ch from hook, (ch 5, sk next 5 ch, dc in next ch) twice, turn — 3 ch-5 loops.

Row 2: Ch 6 (counts as dc, ch 3), sc in 3rd ch of next ch-5 loop, ★ch 3, dc in next dc, ch 3, skip next 2 ch, sc in next ch; rep from ★ once, ch 3, skip next 2 ch, dc in next ch, turn — 6 ch-3 loops.

Row 3: Ch 8 (counts as dc, ch 5), skip next 2 ch-3 loops, ★dc in next dc, ch 5, skip next 2 ch-3 loops; rep from ★ once, Dc in 3rd ch of ch-6 turning ch, turn — 3 ch-5 loops.

Row 4: Rep Row 2.

Rows 5–22: Rep Row 3–4 (9 times)

Row 23: Rep Row 3. Do not fasten off.

Note: If you adjusted the cuff for size, remember that each cotton flower corresponds to four rows in the trellis; add or subtract rows as needed to match the length of the cuff, ending with Row 3 of pattern.

EDGING AND CLASP

With RS of each facing up, place Flower panel over Trellis, matching side edges.

Rnd 1: Ch 1, turn work clockwise to work across long edge of cuff, ★★work 2 sc around next row-end dc on Trellis, sc in first ch of next row-end turning ch, ★working through double thickness of Flower panel and Trellis, sc in first tr of next petal and in ch-3 space on side edge of Trellis, sc in next tr and same ch-3 space, (sc in top of next row-end st on Trellis, 2 sc around the post of same row-end st) 3 times; rep from ★ across, joining all free flower petals on side, work 3 sc in corner st★★, working across short edge of cuff, working through double thickness, sc in each of next 2 tr of next petal and ch-5 loop of Trellis, 3 sc in same ch-5 loop, sc in next tr of next petal and same ch-5 loop of Trellis, sc in next tr of same petal and next ch-5 loop of Trellis, 2 sc in same ch-5 loop, work button loop: ch 12, sl st in 12th ch from hook, ch 1, turn, work 30 sc in ch-12 loop, sl st in first sc to join (button loop complete); continue to work across short edge of cuff, sc in same ch-5 loop, sc in next tr of next petal and same ch-5 loop of trellis, sc in next tr of same petal and next ch of trellis, 3 sc in same ch-5 loop, sc in each of next 2 tr of next petal and same ch-5 loop, 3 sc in corner st, rep from ★★ to ★★ once, omitting button loop on second short side, sl st in first sc to join. Fasten off. Weave in ends.

FINISHING

With the metallic thread and with the RS of cuff facing you, sew the pearl bead (or button) to the bottom of the button loop. To secure the cuff, insert the button loop from the back to the front in ch-5 loop on the opposite end of the cuff, then insert the bead (or button) through the button loop. To care for your cuff, hand-wash it and lay it flat to dry.

END NOTES

Try making the cuff with different colors and different fibers. You can use several strands of regular sewing thread. If you're giving the cuff as a gift, use the favorite colors of the recipient to make it extra-special.

This project was created with

1 ball each of Coats Manila Bay *Cannon* bedspread weight cotton thread in white, and dark beige (MB117), 100% mercerized cotton, 192yd/175m

1 spool each of Coats GmbH *Ophir* Metallic Thread in silver (#301) and gold (#300), 60% viscose/40% polyester, 44y/40m.

Amigurumi Set

Crocheted from metallic black and gold fibers, these serpentine accessories will add an edge to any outfit.

ELIZABETA NEDELJKOVICH-MARTONOSI

HANDCUFF

With A, ch 2.

Row 1: Work 6 sc in 2nd ch from hook, do not sl st to join — 6 sc. Work in a spiral, marking beg of each rnd and moving marker up as work progresses.

Row 2: Work 2 sc in each sc around — 12 sc.

Rows 3–4: Sc in each sc around — 12 sc. Complete last sc with B, drop A to WS to be picked up later.

Rows 5–6: With B, sc in each sc around — 12 sc. Drop B to WS, pick up A.

Rows 7–9: With A, sc in each sc around — 12 sc. Drop A, pick up B.

Stuff with pillow filling after every 1½"/4cm. Do not overstuff, but rather shape the piece so that it is smooth on the inner side and round on the outer side.

Rows 10–54: Rep Rows 5–9 (9 times). At end of last rnd, sl st in next sc to join. Fasten off, leaving a 10"/25cm sewing length.

The last row is the 10th repetition of B. Push beginning end of the snake into the other end, then using yarn needle and sewing length, sew them together.

CHOKER

Work same as Handcuff through Rnd 9.

Stuff with pillow filling after every 1½"/4cm. Do not overstuff, but rather shape the piece so that the piece is smooth on the inner side and round on the outer side.

Rnds 10–84: Rep Rnds 5–9 (15 times).

Rnds 85–88: Rep Rows 5–8.

Rnd 89: ★Skip next sc, sc in next sc; rep from ★ around, sl st in next sc to join — 6 sc. Fasten off, leaving a 5"/12.5cm sewing length. With yarn needle, weave sewing length through last rnd of sts, gather tightly and secure.

FINISHING

Sew one keychain ring to each end of the choker. Insert the end of the chain into one of the keychain rings, and the lobster clasp into the other.

These projects were created with

Park Dyed Yarns WO–12 in Camel, 100 % rayon, and Britanica's Disco Fashion in black and gold lamé (#119), 60% rayon with 40% metalized polyester.

SKILL LEVEL

Easy

FINISHED MEASUREMENTS

Handcuff: 8½"/22cm in circumference

Height: 1"/2.5cm

Choker: 15"/38cm long, excluding chain

Height: 1"/2.5c

YOU WILL NEED

Approx 84yd/77m superfine yarn in old gold (A)

Approx 54yd/49m superfine twined metallic rayon yarn in black and gold lamé (B)

Hook: size 2mm/3

Stitch markers or contrasting yarn for markers

Yarn needle

Pillow filler

Sewing needle

2 keychain rings, 6 mm diameter

3 inches of chain

Lobster clasp

STITCHES USED

Chain stitch (ch)

Single crochet (sc)

Slip stitch (sl st)

GAUGE

6 sts and 6 rows sc = 1"/2.5cm. Tube = approx 1"/2.5cm in diameter

Night Sky Bracelet

dramatic black-and-white boucle yarn gives this distinctive bangle evening allure. The pattern is composed of simple single crochet stitches.

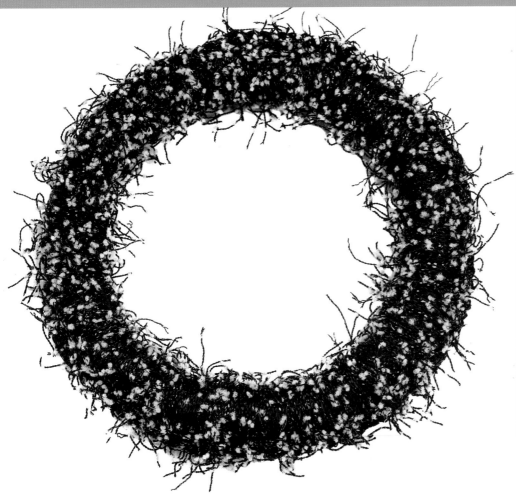

COVERING THE BRACELET

With one strand each of A and B held together as one, make a slip knot and join the yarn around the bangle bracelet, sc closely and evenly around the bracelet, pushing sts along shaft of the bracelet until it's completely covered, sl st in first sc to join. Fasten off, and weave in the ends.

Note to beginners: Habu Kasumi is a textured yarn. It will occasionally catch on your hook or with the other sts, so be patient when working with it. If you pull too hard on the yarn, it may break. Using the tapestry needle, ease up the yarn where it's caught before pulling the stitch tight.

This project was created with

1 ball of Habu *Kasumi* in A-28B in Black (#10), 100% polyester, ½oz/14g = 60yd/54m

1 skein of Rowan Lurex *Shimmer* in Black (#334), 80% viscose, 20% polyester, .9oz/25g = 104yds/95m.

SKILL LEVEL

Easy

FINISHED MEASUREMENTS

Diameter: 3½"/9cm

YOU WILL NEED

60yd/54m single-strand boucle yarn in black and white (A)

104yd/95m light weight lurex shimmer yarn in black (B)

Hook: size 4mm/G-6

Bangle bracelet: ½"/1.3cm diameter

Tapestry needle

STITCHES USED

Slip stitch (sl st)

Single crochet (sc)

GAUGE

Exact gauge is not crucial for this pattern.

Gothic Rose Wristlet

ombining old-fashioned elegance with contemporary chic, this easy-to-crochet band is adorned with classic florets and a vintage button.

BAND

With A, ch 5.

Row 1: Sc in 2nd ch from hook, sc in each ch across, turn 4 sc.

Row 2: Ch 1, sc in each sc across, turn 4 sc.

Rep Row 2 until band measures 8"/20.5cm or ½"/1.3cm longer than circumference of wrist. Fasten off. Weave in ends.

ROSETTE

With B, leaving a sewing length, ch 5, sl st in first ch to form a ring.

Rnd 1: Ch 1, work 11 sc in ring, sl st in first sc to join 11 sc.

Rnd 2: Ch 8 (counts as dc, ch 5), skip first sc, (dc, ch 5) in each sc around, sl st in 3rd ch of turning ch to join 11 ch-5 loops. Fasten off. Weave in ends.

FINISHING

Use the sewing needle and thread to sew the center of the rosette to the center of the band. Then sew the button to the center of the rosette. Sew on the snap, placing it ½"/1.3cm from each end of the band.

This project was created with

1 skein each of The Caron Collection *Watercolours* (equivalant to a worsted weight cotton) in Caribbean (#089) and Mediterranean (#068), 100% puma cotton, 10yd/9m.

SKILL LEVEL

Easy

FINISHED MEASUREMENTS

Band: 8"/20.5cm long x 1"/2.5cm wide

YOU WILL NEED

10yd/9m 3-ply cotton (equivalent to a worsted weight cotton) in seafoam variegated (A)

10yd/9m 3-ply cotton (equivalent to a worsted weight cotton) in blue variegated (B)

Hook: size 4mm/G-6

Yarn needle

Vintage button

Large snap

Sewing needle

Sewing thread in coordinating color

STITCHES USED

Chain stitch (ch)

Slip stitch (sl st)

Single crochet (sc)

Double crochet (dc)

GAUGE

With A, in band pattern, 4 sc = ⅞"/2.2cm.

Victorian Button Rings

these handsome rings may look intricate, but they're incredibly easy to make. Crochet them in your favorite colors, then add antique buttons for a vintage feel.

Note: The instructions are written for size small, with medium and large sizes in parentheses.

RING

Leaving a 12"/30.5cm tail, ch 25 (29, 33).

Rnd 1: Hdc in 3rd ch from hook, ★sl st in next ch, hdc in next ch; rep from ★ across, ending with (hdc, ch 2, hdc) in last ch, working across opposite side of foundation ch, rep from ★ across, ch 2, sl st in top of turning ch. Fasten off leaving a 12"/30.5cm sewing length.

FINISHING

Slide the button onto one of the 12"/30.5cm yarn tails. Bring the other 12"/30.5cm tail through the button going in the opposite direction. With the tapestry needle, weave each tail through the button and fabric to secure it. Apply jeweler's glue to the cut ends.

This project was created with

1 ball of Coats *Opera* (size 10) in Claret (#585), 100% cotton, 1.75oz/50g = 251yd/230m.

SKILL LEVEL

Easy

FINISHED MEASUREMENTS

Small ring: 2"/5cm finger circumference. Ring sizes 6 and 7

Medium ring: 2½"/6.5cm finger circumference. Ring size 8

Large ring: 3"/7.5cm finger circumference. Ring sizes 9 and 10

YOU WILL NEED

Approx 25yd/23m size 10 crochet cotton thread

Hook: size 1.15mm/10 or size needed to obtain gauge

Shank button, ¾"/2cm

Tapestry needle

Jeweler's glue

STITCHES USED

Chain stitch (ch)

Slip stitch (sl st)

Half double crochet (hdc)

GAUGE

11 sts in pattern = 1"/2.5cm

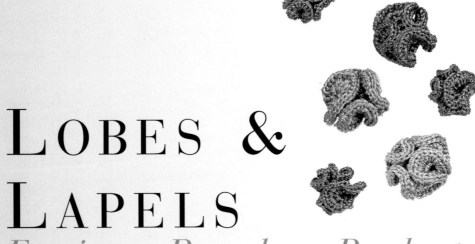

LOBES &
LAPELS

Earrings . Brooches . Pendants

Silver Spirals

DESIGNER · ALEXANDRA CALUB

this opulent earring-and-necklace ensemble pairs handsome silver dangles with pink freshwater pearls. Crocheted from metallic embroidery thread, the spirals are surprisingly simple to stitch.

PATTERN NOTES

The size of thread used for this set is smaller than what's normally used with a size 8 hook. Thus, your stitches will be loose. You may be tempted to hold onto the beads as you work through, but don't. Holding the beads will tighten your stitches and make the beads dangle far from the stitches.

Experiment with color. Try making this set with a different shade of metallic thread. You can also use colored crystals in different hues. Changing colors can dramatically alter the look of your projects. With a few simple variations, you can create an elegant jewelry ensemble for evening or a fun, funky set for daytime wear.

NECKLACE

String 7 beads on thread. Ch 22.

Row 1: Sc in 2nd ch from hook, sc in each ch across, turn — 21 sc.

Row 2: Ch 3 (counts as dc), 4 dc in first sc, 3 sc in next sc, (bsc, 2 sc) in next sc, ★5 dc in next sc, 3 sc in next sc, (bsc, 2 sc) in next sc; rep from ★ across. Fasten off, leaving sewing length. Weave in ends.

Use the needle-nose pliers to open one of the silver rings and attach the ring to the first group of 5-dc. Insert the silver chain through the ring. Then use the needle-nose pliers to attach the lobster lock set to the ends of the chain.

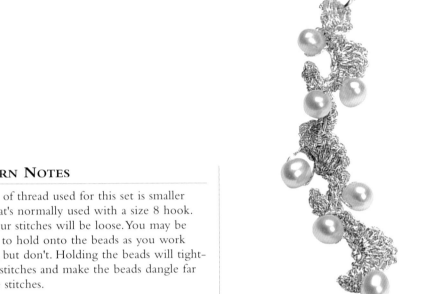

EARRING *(make 2)*

String 5 beads on thread. Ch 16.

Row 1: Sc in 2nd ch from hook, sc in each ch across, turn — 15 sc.

Row 2: Ch 3 (counts as dc), 4 dc in first sc, 3 sc in next sc, (bsc, 2 sc) in next sc, ★5 dc in next sc, 3 sc in next sc, (bsc, 2 sc) in next sc; rep from ★ across. Fasten off, leaving sewing length. Weave in ends.

Use the needle-nose pliers to attach one of the silver rings to the first group of 5-dc. Then attach the fishhook earring wire. Repeat for the other earring.

To care for your set, hand-wash it and let it air-dry.

This project was created with

1 spool of Coats GmbH *Ophir* in Silver (#301), 60% viscose, 40% polyester met., 45yd/40m.

SKILL LEVEL

Intermediate

FINISHED MEASUREMENTS

Earrings: 1¾"/4.5cm long (excluding hooks)

Pendant: 2½"/6.5cm

YOU WILL NEED

Approx 3yd/2.7m silver metallic embroidery thread

Hook: size 1.4mm/8

17 pink freshwater pearl beads, 5mm

Needle-nose pliers

3 silver rings, 5mm diameter

17"/43cm of Korean silver-plated necklace chain

Silver lobster lock set

Darning needle or sharp-pointed needle with eye to fit thread

Silver fishhook earring set

STITCHES USED

Chain stitch (ch)

Slip stitch (sl st)

Single crochet (sc)

Double crochet (dc)

Beaded single crochet (bsc): Slide bead up to work, insert hook in next st, yo, draw yarn through st, yo, draw yarn through 2 loops on hook (Note: bead will appear on back of st).

GAUGE

9 sts = approx 1"/2.5cm.

Crocheted Beads Suite

Create this necklace and earring ensemble, and you'll have a perfect pair—two essential accessories that are incredibly easy to wear.

PATTERN NOTES

A. 1½"/4cm dowel cap covered in light pumpkin silk thread (A) (make 1)

B. 1"/2.5cm bead covered in light pumpkin silk thread (A) (make 3)

C. 1"/2.5cm bead covered in light peach metallic thread (E) (make 1)

D. ⅞"/22.2mm bead covered in light peach metallic thread (E) (make 1)

E. 1"/2.5cm bead covered in dark pumpkin silk thread (B) (make 1)

F. ⅝"/15.9mm bead covered in copper cord (F) (make 3)

G. ⅞"/22.2mm bead covered in copper cord (F) (make 1)

H. 1"/2.5cm bead covered in sienna metallic thread (C) (make 1)

I. ⅞"/22.2mm bead covered in sienna metallic thread (C) (make 1)

J. 1"/2.5cm bead covered in red metallic thread (D) (make 1)

K. ⅞"/22.2mm bead covered in red metallic thread (D) (make 1)

COVER FOR 1½"/4CM BEAD

Ch 10, sl st in first ch to form a ring.

Rnd 1: Ch 1, work 12 sc in ring, do not join — 12 sc. Work in a spiral, marking beg of each rnd and moving marker up as work progresses.

Rnd 2: ★Sc in next sc, 2 sc in next sc; rep from ★ around — 18 sc.

Rnds 3–4: Rep Rnd 2 – 40 sc at end of last rnd.

Rnds 5–15: Sc in each sc around — 40 sc. Weave in beginning tail. Place cover over bead, aligning center hole with bead hole, and continue.

Rnd 16: ★Sc in each of next 2 sc, sc2tog in next 2 sts; rep from ★ around — 30 sc.

Rnd 17: Rep Rnd 16 — 20 sc.

Rnd 18: ★Sc in next sc, sc2tog in next 2 sts; rep from ★ around — 15 sc.

Rnd 19: Sc in each sc around — 15 sc.

Rnd 20: ★Sc in each of next 2 sc, sc2tog in next 2 sts; rep from ★ twice, sc in each of last 3 sc — 12 sc. Fasten off. Weave in ends.

Necklace

SKILL LEVEL

Intermediate

FINISHED MEASUREMENTS

52"/132cm long, not including hanging ribbon

YOU WILL NEED

88yd/80m light pumpkin silk thread (A)

22yd/20m dark pumpkin silk thread (B)

22yd/20m each sienna (C), red (D), light peach (E) metallic thread

33yd/30m copper cord (F)

Hook: size 1.75mm/4 or size needed to obtain gauge

1 wooden dowel cap, 1½"/4cm

7 wooden beads, 1"/2.5cm

4 wooden beads, ⅞"/22mm

3 wooden beads, ⅝"/16mm

4 yd/3.7m of silk ribbon, 1½"/4cm wide, in a coordinating color

Tapestry needle

STITCHES USED

Chain stitch (ch)

Slip stitch (sl st)

Single crochet (sc)

Sc2tog: (Insert hook in next st, yo, draw yarn through st) twice, yo, draw yarn through 3 loops on hook.

GAUGE

10 sts and 10 rnds sc = 1"/2.5cm

COVER FOR 1"/2.5CM BEAD

Ch 6, sl st in first ch to form a ring.

Rnd 1: Ch 1, work 6 sc loosely in ring, do not join — 6 sc. Work in a spiral as before.

Rnd 2: 2 sc in each sc around — 12 sc.

Rnd 3: ★Sc in next sc, 2 sc in next sc; rep from ★ around — 18 sc.

Rnd 4: ★Sc in each of next 2 sc, 2 sc in next sc; rep from ★ around — 24 sc.

Rnds 5–11: Sc in each sc around — 24 sc. Weave in beginning tail. Place cover over bead.

Rnd 12: ★Sc in each of next 2 sc, sc2tog in next 2 sts; rep from ★ around — 18 sc.

Rnd 13: ★Sc in next sc, sc2tog in next 2 sts; rep from ★ around — 12 sc.

Rnd 14: Rep Rnd 13 — 6 sc. Fasten off. Weave in ends.

COVER FOR ⅞"/22.2MM BEAD

Rep Rnds 1–4 of cover for 1"/2.5cm bead.

Rnds 5–10: Sc in each sc around – 24 sc. Weave in beginning tail. Place cover over bead.

Rnd 11: ★Sc in each of next 2 sc, sc2tog in next 2 sts; rep from ★ around — 18 sc.

Rnd 12: ★Sc in next sc, sc2tog in next 2 sts; rep from ★ around — 12 sc.

Rnd 13: Rep Rnd 12 — 6 sc. Fasten off. Weave in ends.

COVER FOR ⅝"/15.9MM BEAD

Rep Rnds 1–3 of cover for 1"/2.5cm bead.

Rnds 4–7: Sc in each sc around — 18 sc. Weave in beginning tail. Place cover over bead.

Rnd 8: ★Sc in next sc, sc2tog in next 2 sts; rep from ★ around — 12 sc.

Rnd 9: Rep Rnd 8 — 6 sc. Fasten off. Weave in ends.

FINISHING

When the 15 beads are completed, cut a 60"/152cm length of the silk ribbon and thread it through the tapestry needle. Thread bead H down the ribbon approximately 26"/66cm and tie an overhand knot on each side of the bead. Tie another overhand knot 2½"/6.5cm up from the last knot. Thread beads F, K, and B onto the ribbon, placing a knot between them and after B. Tie another overhand knot 2½"/6.5cm up from the last knot. Next, thread beads C, G, and B as before (see diagram). Repeat for the opposite side of the necklace, threading beads J, B, I, E, F, D, F. Place two 30"/76cm-lengths of ribbon over the center of the main ribbon, between beads J and H, and thread the tails through the hole of the 1½"/38mm bead. Tie an overhand knot with all 4 lengths under this bead to secure it. Tie the finished necklace with a square knot at the back of the neck.

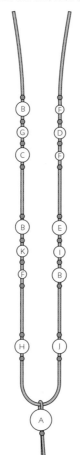

Earrings

FINISHED MEASUREMENTS

2¼"/5.5cm long

YOU WILL NEED

Approx 35yd/30m metallic thread (equivalent to #10 crochet thread) in each of the following colors: light copper (A), dark copper (B)

Approx 35yd/30m silk thread (equivalent to #10 crochet thread) in pumpkin (C)

Hook: size 1.5mm/7 or size needed to obtain gauge

2 wooden beads, 10mm

2 wooden beads, 12mm

2 wooden beads, 16mm

2 faceted glass beads, 6mm

2 headpins, 3"/7.5cm

Needle-nose pliers

2 ear wires

GAUGE

Approx 10 sts = 1"/2.5cm; first 5 rnds of large bead = ¾"/2cm in diameter. Take time to check your gauge.

SMALL BEAD *(make 2)*

With A, ch 2.

Rnd 1: Work 4 sc in 2nd ch from hook, do not join — 4 sc. Work in a spiral, marking beg of each rnd and moving marker up as work progresses.

Rnd 2: 2 sc in each sc around — 8 sc.

Rnd 3: ★2 sc in next sc, sc in next sc; rep from ★ around — 12 sc.

Rnd 4: Sc in each sc around — 12 sc. Insert 10mm bead into covering.

Rnd 5: ★Sc2tog in next 2 sc, sc in next sc; rep from ★ around — 8 sc.

Rnd 6: ★Sc2tog in next 2 sc; rep from ★ around — 4 sc. Fasten off. Weave in ends.

MEDIUM BEAD (MAKE 2)

With B, work same as small bead through Rnd 3 — 12 sc.

Rnd 4: ★2 sc in next sc, sc in each of next 2 sc; rep from ★ around — 16 sc.

Rnd 5: Sc in each sc around — 16 sc. Insert 12mm bead into covering.

Rnd 6: ★Sc2tog in next 2 sc, sc in each of next 2 sc; rep from ★ around — 12 sc.

Rnd 7: ★Sc2tog in next 2 sc, sc in next sc; rep from ★ around — 8 sc.

Rnd 8: ★Sc2tog in next 2 sc; rep from ★ around — 4 sc. Fasten off. Weave in ends.

LARGE BEAD *(make 2)*

With C, work same as medium bead through Rnd 4 — 16 sc.

Rnd 5: ★2 sc in next sc, sc in each of next 2 sc; rep from ★ 4 times, sc in next sc — 21 sc.

Rnd 6: Sc in each sc around — 21 sc. Insert 16mm bead into covering.

Rnd 7: ★Sc2tog in next 2 sc, sc in each of next 2 sc; rep from ★ 4 times, sc in next sc — 16 sc.

Rnd 8: Rep Rnd 7 — 12 sc.

Rnd 9: ★Sc2tog in next 2 sc, sc in next sc; rep from ★ around — 8 sc.

Rnd 10: ★Sc2tog in next 2 sc; rep from ★ around — 4 sc. Fasten off. Weave in ends.

FINISHING

Place the glass bead on the headpin, then add the large, medium, and small covered beads. With the needle-nose pliers, bend the pin toward the beads ¼"/6mm above the last bead. Then wrap the end of the pin around itself three times to form a loop and pinch it to secure. Use the needle-nose pliers to open the loop of the ear wire, then insert the ear wire into the earring loop and close the loop with the pliers to secure it. Repeat this process to make the second earring.

These projects were created with

4 spools of Kreinik Silk *Serica* in light pumpkin (#2063) (A), 3-ply, 100% filament silk, 22yd/20m

1 spool of Kreinik Silk *Serica* in dark pumpkin (#2066) (B), 3-ply, 100% filament silk, 22yd/20m

2 spools each of Kreinik Fine Braid (#8) metallic thread in vintage sienna (#152V) (C), red flamenco (#3503) (D), and light peach (#9192) (E), 11yd/10m

3 spools of Kreinik metallic cord in copper cord (#021C), 11yd/10m

4 yd M&J Trimmings hand-dyed silk ribbon, (1½"/3.8cm) in Echinacea (#25179)

1 spool each of Kreinik's Fine (#8) Braid (#021C), Copper Cord (A), (#3503) red flamenco (B), 11yd/10m

1 spool of Kreinik's Silk *Serica* (#2063), Light Pumpkin (C), 11yd/10m.

Hyperbolic Beads

don't let the fancy name fool you! The design of these distinctive beads is based on a geometric concept called the hyperbolic plane. With a few jewelry findings and these sensational pieces, you can create a cutting-edge necklace and earrings set in an afternoon.

DESIGNER · PAM SHORE

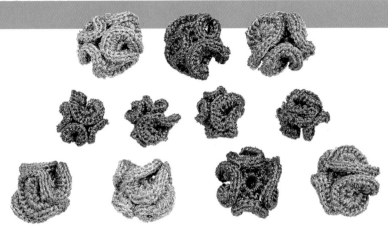

PATTERN NOTES

Hints for working with metallic floss: Knot the ends. Keep a tight tension to avoid splitting the floss, but not so tight that the hook won't go into a stitch. Working slowly, stretch the previous round slightly to avoid missing stitches. The final shape can be modified by manipulating the curves.

Directions for separating floss for small balls: Stand in good light. Find the end of the skein of floss and hold it between the thumb and first finger of your right hand with the skein across your palm. Remove the label and let the skein fall to the floor. Grab one strand (careful: each "strand" is actually two) and pull it slowly. The top of the skein will curl up in the palm of your right hand. Keep pulling carefully, letting the bottom of the skein untwist. Repeat this process until one strand is free, then lay it aside. Repeat the process for the second strand. A four-strand length should remain in your right hand. Knot the end between your thumb and finger. Straighten out the floss, knot the other end, and wind it onto a piece of the cardboard. Combine the two single strands, then fold them in half to make a four-strand length. Then knot the ends and wind the length onto the other piece of cardboard.

LARGE BALL (for necklace)

With larger hook and 6-strand of embroidery floss (use floss as packaged, unseparated)

Rnd 1: Leaving 1"/2.5cm tail, ch 6, sl st in first ch to form a ring.

Rnd 2: Ch 1, 12 sc in ring (working over tail), sl st in first sc to join, turn. Clip tail close to sts.

Rnd 3: Ch 1, 3 sc in each sc around, sl st in first sc to join, turn.

Rnd 4: Rep Rnd 3.

Rnd 5: Sl st in each sc around. Fasten off. Weave in end.

SMALL BALL (make 2 for earrings)

With smaller hook and 4 strands of embroidery floss, work same as large ball through Rnd 4. Fasten off. Weave in end.

FINISHING

String the large ball onto the neck ring, through the center hole. String one small ball onto each earring hoop, positioning the balls as desired. Use the needle-nose pliers to bend up the ends of the hoops.

This project was created with

2 skeins of DMC Metallic Floss *Light Effects* Precious Metals, metallic thread, 100% polyester, 8.7 yds/8m. Colors used to make various balls: copper (E301), white gold (E677), light gold (E3821). Yardage needed: 1 skein for 1 large ball (necklace); 1 skein, divided, for 2 small balls (earrings).

SKILL LEVEL

Intermediate

FINISHED MEASUREMENTS

Large ball: 1"/2.5cm

Small ball: ¾"/2cm

YOU WILL NEED

8.7yd/8m of 6-strand metallic embroidery floss for necklace

6.5yd/6m of 4 strands of metallic embroidery floss for 2 earrings

Hooks: 2mm/3 and 1.5mm/7

2 pieces of cardboard, each 2"/5cm x 2"/5cm

Neck ring

2 silver-colored wire hoops for earrings, 20mm diameter

Needle-nose pliers

STITCHES USED

Chain st (ch)

Slip stitch (sl st)

Single crochet (sc)

GAUGE

With the larger hook and 6-strand embroidery floss, large ball = 1"/2.5cm in diameter. With the smaller hook and 4 strands of embroidery floss, small ball = ¾"/2cm in diameter.

Samba Earrings

these impossible-
to-ignore earrings
offer abundant color and
plenty of texture. Put them
on, and you'll be prepared for
a party.

PATTERN NOTES

Push the ring to the side and back of the work as you crochet the clusters in Rnd 3. Move sl st around the ring to stretch and separate them as you work the last stitches of Rnd 3.

Motif (make 2)

Ch 5, join with sl st in first ch to form a ring.

Rnd 1: Ch 4, 19 tr in ring, covering tail as you work, sl st in top of beg ch —20 tr.

Rnd 2: Ch 7 (counts as tr, ch 3), (tr, ch 3) in each tr around, sl st in 4th ch of beg ch-7 to join - 20 ch-3 loops.

Rnd 3 (joining rnd): Sl st to center of first ch-3 loop, ch 2 (counts as hdc), hdc in same space (counts as first bobble), ★ch 1, sl st in 2"/5cm silver ring, ch 1★★, bobble in next ch-3 loop; rep from ★ around, ending last rep at ★★, sl st in top of beg ch-2. Fasten off. Weave in ends.

FINISHING

Use the needle-nose pliers to open one of the jump rings, then attach the jump ring to the 2"/5cm ring at any point. Slightly open one of the ear wires and attach it to the jump ring. Sew one 4mm silver bead to the center of each motif.

This project was created with

1 spool of Kreinik's Very Fine (#4) Braid in Blue Samba (#3506), 11yd/10m.

SKILL LEVEL

Intermediate

FINISHED MEASUREMENTS

Diameter: 2"/5cm

YOU WILL NEED

Approx 11yd/10m metallic thread (equivalent to #20 crochet thread) in light blue

Hook: size 1.25mm/9 or size needed to obtain gauge

Tapestry needle

2 silver rings, 2"/5cm diameter

Needle-nose pliers

2 silver jump rings, 5mm diameter

2 earring wires

2 silver beads, 4mm

STITCHES USED

Slip stitch (sl st)

Half double crochet (hdc)

Treble crochet (tr)

Bobble: (Yo, insert hook in next space, yo, draw yarn through loop) twice in same loop, draw through all 5 loops on hook.

GAUGE

Rnd 1 = ¾"/2cm in diameter. Motif = 2"/5cm in diameter.

Oh-So-Fruity Earrings

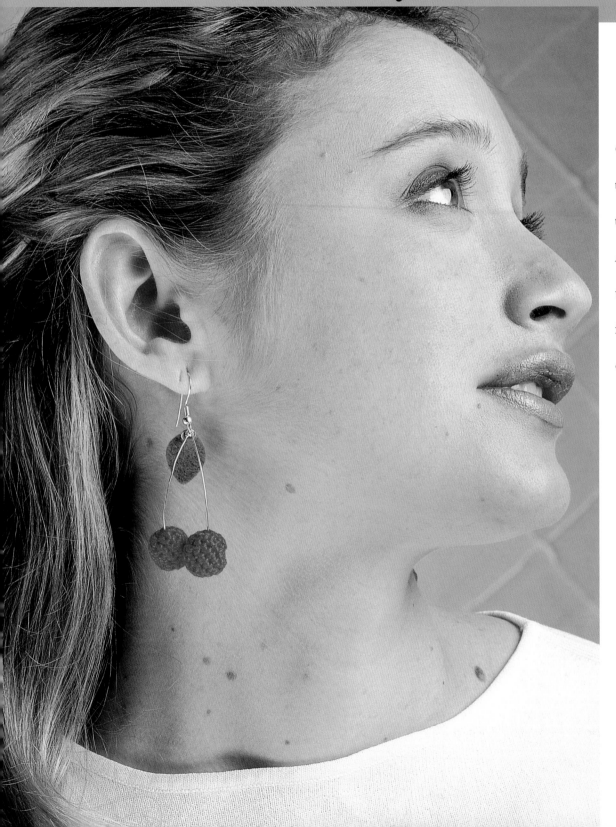

add an
infusion
of color and fun
to any outfit with
these cheery earrings.
Assembling the set
using jump rings and
felt is as easy as
cherry pie!

CHERRY *(make 4)*

With the full 6 strands of embroidery floss, ch 4, sl st in first ch to form a ring.

Rnd 1: Ch 1, sc in each ch around, do not join. Work in a spiral.

Rnd 2: 2 sc in each sc around — 8 sc.

Rnd 3: ★Sc in next sc, 2 sc in next sc; rep from ★ around — 12 sc.

Rnd 4: Sc in each sc around — 12 sc.

Rnd 5: ★Sc in next sc, sc2tog in next 2 sts; rep from ★ around — 8 sc.

At this point, insert the pompom into the cherry. The top of the pompom "fuzz" will stick out of the top. The final rounds are done around the pompom and may be a little tricky to execute at first.

Rnd 6: ★Sc2tog in next 2 sts; rep from ★ around — 4 sc.

Rnd 7: Sc in each sc around. Fasten off. Weave in ends.

LEAVES

Cut three leaf shapes out of the felt, two of them roughly ⅞"/2.2cm long and ½"/1cm wide, and the other slightly smaller, about ⅝"1.6cm long and ⅜"/1cm wide. The tip end of each leaf should be pointed; the base end of each leaf should be slightly wider and rounded.

Use the round-nose pliers to open up each jump ring. The jump rings should go through the two holes in each leaf, forcing the leaves to hold a three-dimensional shape. Fold each leaf in half and pinch each one at its wider end.

Then push the tapestry needle into each of the folded leaves at the wider end, going through the felt twice. Then back the needle out and push the open end of each jump ring through the holes just created. (Note: Sometimes it's easier to "follow" the needle out of the hole rather than pulling it all the way out and trying to find the hole again.)

Slip each of the jump rings through the rings on the bottom of each ear wire and close them using the needle-nose pliers. Repeat the steps for each leaf, placing the larger leaf on one ear wire and the other two leaves on the other ear wire.

STEMS

For each cherry, push the tapestry needle into the cherry, going from the top (where the last round is) to the bottom (where the first round is) and making sure to go through the center of the pompom. If you can't tell the top from the bottom anymore, don't worry about it.

Slowly remove the needle. As you pull it out, feed the end of one of the headpins into the hole. This takes a little practice. If the process seems unusually difficult, try working with a larger needle.

Push the cherry all the way down the headpin, until the bottom of the headpin is just barely visible at what is now the bottom of the cherry. Give the headpin a short tug to make sure that it's going through the pompom securely and not merely sitting in the fluff off to the side. Then use your fingers to add a slight curve to the headpin.

Use the round-nose pliers to make a small loop in the end of the headpin and hook it onto the ear wire before closing. Attach two stem-and-cherries to each ear wire.

This project was created with

1 skein of DMC 6-strand embroidery floss in Red (#666), 100% cotton, 8.7yd/8m.

SKILL LEVEL

Intermediate

FINISHED MEASUREMENTS

Cherries: Approx ½"/1.3cm in diameter

Finished earring: Approx 1¾"/4.5cm in length

YOU WILL NEED

8.7yd/8m of 6-strand cotton embroidery floss in red

Hook: size 1.4mm/8

4 red pompoms, 10mm

Size 14 tapestry needle (or similar size)

Piece of green felt, 2" square

Round-nose pliers

3 silver jump rings, 4mm

2 silver or silver-plate ear wires

4 silver or silver-plate headpins, 2"/5cm long

STITCHES USED

Chain stitch (ch)

Single crochet (sc)

Sc2tog: (Insert hook in next st, yo, draw yarn through st) twice, yo, draw yarn through 3 loops on hook.

GAUGE

Exact gauge is not crucial for this project. Tighter stitches will yield smaller cherries and vice-versa.

Cherry = Approx ½"/1.3cm in diameter.

Bee & Daisy Brooches

p in one of these

adorable accessories

to your lapel, and you're bound to

cause a buzz.

DESIGNER ·
ELIZABETA NEDELJKOVICH-MARTONOSI

BEE'S BODY

Starting at tail end, with A, ch 2.

Row 1: Work 6 sc in 2nd ch from hook, sl st in first sc to join — 6 sc.

Rnd 2: Ch 1, 2 sc in each sc around, sl st in first sc to join — 12 sc. Drop A to WS to be picked up later, join B.

Rnd 3: With B, ch 1, sc in each sc around, sl st in first sc to join — 12 sc. Drop B to WS, pick up A.

Rnd 4: With A, ch 1, sc in each sc around, sl st in first sc to join — 12 sc.

Rnds 5–8: Rep Rows 3–4 (twice).

Rows 9–12: With A, ch 1, sc in each sc around, sl st in first sc to join — 12 sc. Stuff the filling in now, because it will begin to narrow in the next round.

Row 13: Ch 1, *skip next sc, sc in next sc; rep from * around, sl st in first sc to join — 6 sc. Fasten off, leaving a 5"/12.5cm sewing length. With the yarn needle, weave the sewing length through the last rnd of sts, gather them tightly and secure.

BEE'S WING (make 2)

Starting at tip, with C, ch 2.

Rnd 1: Work 6 sc in 2nd ch from hook, sl st in first sc to join — 6 sc.

Rnd 2: Ch 1, 2 sc in each sc around, sl st in first sc to join — 12 sc.

Rnds 3–7: Ch 1, sc in each sc around, sl st in first sc to join — 12 sc. Fasten off, leaving a 5"/12.5cm sewing length.

Flatten the wings and sew them to the top of the body symmetrically as pictured. Sew the beads on the head for the eyes. Then sew the pin back lengthwise onto the belly.

FLOWER CENTER

With D, ch 2.

Rnd 1: Work 7 sc in 2nd ch from hook, sl st in first sc to join — 7 sc.

Rnd 2: Ch 1, 2 sc in each sc around, sl st in first sc to join — 14 sc.

Rnd 3: Ch 1, 2 sc in first sc, *sc in each of next 2 sc, 2 sc in next sc; rep from * 3 times, sc in last sc, sl st in first sc to join — 19 sc.

Rnds 4–5: Ch 1, sc in each sc around, sl st in first sc to join — 19 sc.

Rnd 6: Ch 1, *sc in each of next 2 sc, skip next sc; rep from * 5 times, sc in last sc, sl st in first sc to join — 13 sc. Insert the filling now.

Rnd 7: Ch 1, *sc in next sc, skip next sc; rep from * 5 times, sc in last sc, sl st in first sc to join — 7 sc.

Rnd 8: Ch 1, *sc in next sc, skip next sc; rep from * twice, sc in last sc, sl st in first sc to join — 4 sc. Fasten off, leaving a 5"/12.5cm sewing length. With yarn needle, weave sewing length through last rnd of sts, gather tightly and secure.

FLOWER PETAL (make 5)

Starting at tip of petal, with C, ch 2.

Rnd 1: Work 6 sc in 2nd ch from hook, sl st in first sc to join — 6 sc.

Rnd 2: Ch 1, 2 sc in each sc around — 12 sc.

Rnd 3: Ch 1, *sc in next sc, 2 sc in each of next 2 sc; rep from * around, sl st in first sc to join — 20 sc.

Rnds 4–7: Ch 1, sc in each sc around, sl st in first sc to join — 20 sc. Fasten off, leaving a 5"/12.5cm sewing length.

Flatten the petals and the flower center. Sew the petals around the circumference of the flower center. Sew any extra thread into the centerpiece, then sew the pin back to the underside of the flower center.

This project was created with

1 skein each of Lion Brand *Microspun* yarn in Ebony (#153) (A), Buttercup (#158) (B), French Vanilla (#98) (C), and Mango (#186) (D), 100% micro-fiber acrylic, 2.5oz/70g = 168yd/154m.

SKILL LEVEL

Easy

FINISHED MEASUREMENTS

Bee: 2½"/6.5cm x 2"/5cm

Flower: 4"/10cm in diameter

YOU WILL NEED

For the bee's body: Approx 5yd/4m microfiber acrylic in black (A)

Approx 1½yd/1m microfiber acrylic in yellow (B)

For the bee's wings and the flower petals: 40yd/37m microfiber acrylic in cream (C)

For the flower center: 4yd/3m microfiber acrylic in orange (D)

Hook: size 3.25mm/D-3

Yarn needle

Pillow filler

Sewing needle with a large eye

4 seed beads, 3mm

2 pin backs

STITCHES USED

Chain stitch (ch)

Single crochet (sc)

Slip stitch (sl st)

GAUGE

6 sts and 6 rows sc = 1"/2.5cm. First 2 rnds of flower center = 1"/2.5cm.

Morning Tide Brooch

this bold **t**brooch is as sparkling as a sunrise. Seed beads give it a special luster.

SKILL LEVEL

Easy

FINISHED MEASUREMENTS

Diameter: 1¾"/4.5cm

4"/10cm long before joining into a circle

YOU WILL NEED

20yd/18.4m of 3-ply embroidery floss in blue-green variegated

Hook: size 4mm/G-6

Beading floss

Beading needle

Tube of size 8 seed beads (approximately 100 beads)

1"/2.5cm steel pin back

Tapestry needle

Sewing needle

STITCHES USED

Beaded chain stitch (bch): Slide bead up close to work, yo, draw yarn through loop on hook.

Slip stitch (sl st)

Bead slip stitch (bsl st): Slide bead up close to work, insert hook in next st, yo, draw yarn through st and loop on hook.

GAUGE

Exact gauge is not crucial for this pattern.

STRINGING BEADS

Cut a 3"/8cm piece of the beading floss, thread it through the beading needle, and tie the ends of the floss together. Thread the eye of the floss with embroidery floss and carefully pick up 70 beads, pushing them down to the end of the embroidery floss as you work.

PIN

With embroidery floss, bch 6, sl st in first ch to form a ring.

Rnd 1: ★Push hook through loop on which the first bead is fastened and flip bead to the RS of the work, with yarn over the top of this bead, bsl st in next st; rep from ★ around, do not sl st to join. Work in spiral.

Rep Rnd 1 until tube measures 4"/10cm from beginning. Fasten off leaving a long tail.

FINISHING

Using the sewing needle, weave the tail through the first stitch of the center ring and pull it tight. Weave it back and forth between the first and last rounds, working through the sts on which the beads rest. Pull the tail tight with each stitch. After the circle is formed and fully stitched, weave the tail through the center of the rope and cut off any excess. Using the beading floss and the sewing needle, sew the pin back to the top back of the circle.

This project was created with

2 skeins of The Caron Collection *Watercolors* Embroidery Floss in Caribbean (#809), 10yd/9.2m.

Flowering Vine Earrings

a delicate daytime accessory, a perfect addition for evening, these earrings will freshen up any outfit, no matter what the hour.

FLOWER (make 6)

With A, ch 5, sl st in first ch to form a ring.

Rnd 1: ★Ch 2, 2 dc in ring, ch 2, sl st in ring; rep from ★ 5 times — 5 petals. Fasten off. Weave in ends.

LEAF (make 8)

With B, ch 8.

Rnd 1: Sc in 2nd ch from hook, hdc in each of next 2 ch, dc in next ch, tr in next ch, dc in next ch, (hdc, sc, hdc) in last ch, working across opposite side of foundation ch, dc in next ch, tr in next ch, dc in next ch, hdc in each of next 2 ch, (hdc, sc) in last ch, sl st in first sc to join. Fasten off. Weave in ends.

FINISHING

Cut the piece of chain into two 1"/2.5cm pieces. Use the needle-nose pliers to open one of the jump rings, then slip the jump ring through the end of one of the leaves and attach it to one end of the chain. Close the jump ring. Alternating between flowers and leaves, continue to attach each piece, working your way up the chain. Then attach the top of the chain to the ear wire.

Repeat these steps to assemble the matching earring.

This project was created with

1 ball of Aunt Lydia's Classic Crochet Thread in White (#1), 100% mercerized cotton, 400yd/366m

1 ball of J&P Coats Royale Classic Crochet Thread in Frosty Green (#661), 100% mercerized cotton, 350yd/320m

SKILL LEVEL

Advanced Beginner

FINISHED MEASUREMENTS

Flowers: ½"/1.3cm in diameter

Leaves: ¾"/2cm long

YOU WILL NEED

6yd/5.5m size 10 crochet thread in white (A)

8yd/7.5m size 10 crochet thread in green (B)

Hook: size 1.75mm/4

2"/5cm of medium silver chain

Wire cutters

14 jump rings, 4mm diameter

Needle-nose pliers

Earring hooks or your choice of earring findings

STITCHES USED

Chain st (ch)

Slip stitch (sl st)

Single crochet (sc)

Half double crochet (hdc)

Double crochet (dc)

Treble crochet (tr)

GAUGE

Flowers = ½"/1.3cm in diameter.

Leaf = ¾"/2cm long.

Ear Doilies

a tradition, in miniature.
The classic doily gets
updated into a fun,
fashionable accessory.
Make these earrings with
one color of thread, or do
a two-tone version.

SKILL LEVEL

Intermediate

FINISHED MEASUREMENTS

Motif: 1½"/3.8cm diameter

YOU WILL NEED

For single-color earrings: 9 yards of bedspread weight crochet cotton thread, size 10 in green (A)

For two-tone earrings: 3yd/3m of bedspread weight crochet cotton thread, size 10 in aqua (B); 6yd/6m of bedspread weight crochet cotton thread, size 10 in brown (C)

Hook: size 1.8mm/6

Needle-nose pliers

Ear wires, or your choice of earring findings

Fabric stiffener

STITCHES USED

Chain stitch (ch)

Slip stitch (sl st)

Single crochet (sc)

Half double crochet (hdc)

Double crochet (dc)

GAUGE

Motif = 1½"/3.8cm in diameter

SINGLE-COLOR EARRING *(make 2)*

With A, ch 3

Rnd 1: Work 11 hdc in 3rd ch from hook, sl st in top of beginning ch-3 — 12 hdc.

Rnd 2: Ch 4 (counts as dc, ch 1), (dc, ch 1) in each hdc around, sl st in 3rd ch of beginning ch to join — 12 ch-1 spaces.

Rnd 3: Sl st in first ch-1 space, ch 6 (counts as dc, ch 3), (dc, ch 3) in each ch-1 space around, sl st in 3rd ch of turning ch to join — 12 ch-3 loops.

Rnd 4: Sl st in first ch-3 loop, (4 sc, sl st) in same ch-3 loop, (sl st, 4 sc, sl st) in each ch-4 loop around, sl st in first sl st to join. Fasten off. Weave in ends.

TWO-TONE EARRING *(make 2)*

Work same as single-color earring, working Rnds 1 and 2 with B. Fasten off B, join C. Work Rnds 3 and 4 with C. Fasten off. Weave in ends.

FINISHING

Use the needle-nose pliers to attach one of the ear wires to the center sc of one of the petals in the last round. The earrings should maintain their shape, but they can be stiffened with the fabric stiffener. See page 124 for instructions on applying fabric stiffener.

This project was created with

1 ball of Aunt Lydia's Classic Crochet Cotton Thread in Wasabi Green (#397), 100% mercerized cotton, 350yd/320m

1 ball of Aunt Lydia's Classic Crochet Cotton Thread in Fudge Brown (#0131), 100% mercerized cotton, 350yd/320m

1 ball of Aunt Lydia's Classic Crochet Cotton Thread in Aqua Blue (#0450), 100% mercerized cotton, 350yd/320m

Posy Brooches

these bright, whimsical brooches are simple to make using soft wool yarn and a few pin backs. The felting process gives the posies extra texture and dimension.

DESIGNER · MARTY MILLER

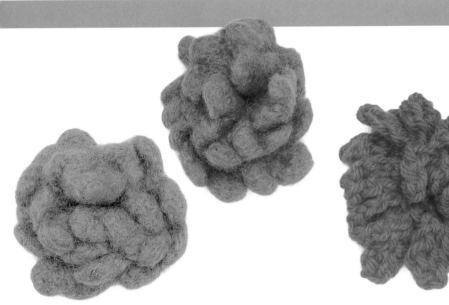

PATTERN NOTES

Directions are written for the small flower. Changes for medium and large flowers are in parentheses.

POSY

With your choice of color, ch 2.

Rnd 1: Work 6 sc in 2nd ch from hook, sl st in front loop of first sc to join — 6 sc.

Rnd 2: Working in front loops only, ch 3 (5, 7), sl st in first sc, ★ch 3 (5, 7), sl st in next sc, ch 3 (5, 7) sl st in same sc; rep from from ★ around, ending with ch 3 (5, 7) sl st in first sl st to join — 12 ch-3 (5, 7) loops.

Rnd 3: Working in back loops only, sl st into back loop of first sc in Rnd 1, ch 5 (7, 9), sl st in first sc of Rnd 1, ★ch 5 (7, 9) sl st in next sc, ch 5(7, 9) sl st in same sc; rep from ★ around, ending with ch 5 (7, 9) sl st in first sl st to join — 12 ch-5 (7, 9) loops. Fasten off. Weave in ends.

FINISHING

Following the instructions on page 123, felt the flower in washing machine. When the flower has felted to your satisfaction, rinse it in a sink with cold water, and pull the petals away from each other. Squeeze the water out of the flower, and put it on a rack or flat surface to dry.

When the flower is dry, use fabric glue to glue on the pin back, or attach the safety pin to the back of the flower.

This project was created with

1 skein each of Lion Brand *Lion* Wool in Dark Teal (#178), Rose (#140), Lemongrass (#132), Pumpkin (#133), Goldenrod (#187), 100% Wool, 3oz/85g = 158yds/144m

1 skein of Lion Brand *Lion* Wool in Autumn Sunset (#201), 100% Wool, 3oz/85g = 143yds/131m.

SKILL LEVEL

Easy

MEASUREMENTS BEFORE FELTING

Approx 3¾–4"/9.5-10cm (small), 4½"/11.5cm (medium), 5"/12.5cm (large)

YOU WILL NEED

Approx 14yd/13m worsted weight 100% wool yarn to make the large flower

Approx 12yd/11m worsted weight 100% wool yarn to make the medium flower

Approx 10yd/9m worsted weight 100% wool yarn to make the small flower

Hook: size 10mm/N-15

Tapestry needle

Pin backs or safety pins without coils

Fabric glue

STITCHES USED

Chain stitch (ch)

Slip stitch (sl st)

Single crochet (sc)

GAUGE

Exact gauge is not crucial for this pattern.

Crochet Basics

Tool & Materials

to make the gorgeous projects in this book, you'll use basic crochet techniques as well as simple jewelry-making procedures. Along with your crochet supplies, there are some extra items you'll need to put the projects together. This section will get you acquainted with the tools and materials necessary to create stylish crocheted chokers, bracelets, earrings, and more.

The Hook

The key to any crochet project is, of course, the hook. The size of the stitches you make is determined by the diameter of your hook. Whether you use an aluminum, plastic, or wooden hook is a matter of personal preference. What matters most is the size of the hook, since it determines the stitch size and, to some extent, the gauge (number of stitches per inch) your pattern is based on.

In the directions for each project in this book and for any other crochet pattern you might work on, you'll be instructed to use a specific hook size. For projects that call for crochet thread or very fine yarn, you'll need a steel crochet hook. Steel hooks are the smallest type of crochet hook. They're generally about five inches long and range in thickness from .90mm (size 14) to 2.7mm (size 00).

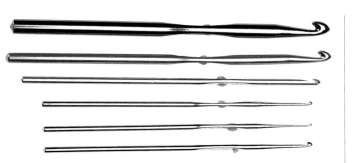

There are three different systems of hook sizes. The Continental (European) system uses millimeters, the U.S. (American) system uses a combination letter/number system, and the United Kingdom uses a numeric system. The hook sizes listed in the projects are of the Continental and U.S. systems (see page 127). For standard crochet hooks, the higher the number or letter, the larger the hook. For steel hooks, which have only an identifying number, the opposite is true—the higher the number, the smaller the hook.

Yarn

Variety, luxury, and novelty are some of the buzzwords you encounter when reading about yarn today. The range of different types of yarn is, simply put, mind-boggling. If you've never shopped for yarn or fibers, you may easily be overwhelmed as you look for material for a specific project (pleasantly so, I might add). Give in to the addictive pleasure of acquisition; don't resist it! After all, you can always find a way to use your impulsive purchases sooner or later.

Each project in this book lists a generic yarn type to use. In addition, each project lists the manufacturer, style, and color of the specific yarn used to create the project. Pay

attention to the type of yarn specified for each project and, if you wish to use a yarn other than the one the designer used (see Substituting Yarn on page 000), look for that type of yarn.

Crochet Thread

Once reserved for frilly pieces like doilies, hats, and baby wear, crochet thread is now commonly used in contemporary crochet patterns. These fine, thin threads are available in various sizes and shades, compositions, and quantities. The threads are sized by weight, and each weight is identified by a number. The lower the number, the thicker the thread. For example, size 3 is a heavier thread than size 8. The most commonly used thread is size 10. Very fine threads, including sizes 30 and 40, are ideal for lacey projects but are used less frequently.

The crochet threads used in this book include sizes 3, 10, 20, and 30. Size 3 comes in a variety of thread compositions, including 100% cotton, microfiber cotton, denim, linen cotton, wool cotton, and metallics. Size 10 is available in 100% mercerized cotton. Premium quality threads

in sizes 10, 20 and 30 are also available, made from 100% double mercerized, combed cotton.

For the purposes of this book, yarn or thread are catchall terms for any fiberlike material used for crochet, even when you're crocheting with ribbon, cloth, or other materials. Keep in mind that a few of the pieces call for uncommon fibers like fishing line and polyester cable cord (the kind typically used in upholstery projects). These fibers are treated just like yarn or thread in the instructions.

Crochet Extras

Scissors, especially small ones with sharp points, are indispensable tools for any crochet project. Breaking yarn is not an efficient way to cut yarn. Always use scissors.

Stitch markers are handy when you need to mark the end of a row in your work or a specific stitch within a row. If you don't wish to purchase stitch markers, use a safety pin or a short length of contrasting yarn to mark your spot.

Rulers and cloth **tape measures** with both standard and metric measurements are useful tools that you probably already have. You will use these tools to measure your work as you progress, to check your gauge (see page 125), and to measure finished pieces as you finish and block them.

Rustproof **pins** of all types—straight pins, T-pins, and safety pins—all have their uses. Make absolutely sure that any type of pin you choose to use is rustproof. T-pins are useful for blocking (see page 126) and safety pins can be used as stitch markers. Straight pins are great for securing

crocheted pieces together as you stitch them and later as you block them.

Tapestry needles with large eyes and blunt points are necessary for finishing a completed crochet project. Using a plastic or metal needle is a matter of preference. Use them to weave loose yarn ends back into your stitches, or to sew together the seams of a garment.

Additional Materials

Here's a rundown of other supplies you should have on hand to make the fabulous projects that follow. Don't be intimidated by the list! Most of these items are basic materials that you probably have already.

■ *Jewelry Tools and Findings*

Needle-nose pliers (also known as long-nose pliers) have a flat inner surface and jaws that taper to a pointed end. Because of their spear-like tip, needle-nose pliers can slip into tight spaces. Be sure to use a pair with a smooth edge on the inside of the jaws—pliers with a serrated inside edge can damage wire.

Round-nose pliers feature cylindrical jaws that taper to a very fine point. They're great for making loops and curves in wire.

Jeweler's wire cutters have very sharp blades that come to a point. One side of the tool leaves a V-shaped cut, while the other side leaves a flat, or "flush," cut.

■ *Findings*

Findings are components, like ear wires or necklace clasps, that hold jewelry together. They're usually made of metal. Some of the most basic findings, including the ones that follow, are used in this book.

Clasps connect wire ends to keep a necklace or bracelet in place. A clasp can be composed of one or two parts and will contain a loop so that you can attach it to your beading string. There are dozens of different types.

Box clasps have one half that's comprised of a hollow box. The other half is a tab that clicks into the box to lock the clasp.

Lobster-claw clasps are spring-activated clasps that are shaped like their name.

Magnetic clasps use powerful magnets to make the connection between one half of the clasp and the other. Use them only with fairly lightweight pieces.

Toggle clasps have one half that looks like a ring with a loop attached to it, while the other half resembles a bar. Pass the bar through the ring; once the bar lays parallel on top of the ring, you've secured the clasp.

Ear wires are the findings you use to make pierced earrings. They include a jump ring-like loop onto which you can add an earring dangle. They come in different shapes, including French ear wires, which look like upside-down U shapes, and hoops, which are simply rounds of thin wire with a catch to hold them in place on the ear.

Head pins are used for stringing beads to make dangles. Simple head pins are made with straight wire with a tiny disk at one end to hold beads in place.

Simple wire circles of various sizes, **jump rings** are split along their circumference. They're ideal for connecting a pendant to a necklace or a clasp to a bracelet.

A **bail** is a metal loop used to attach a pendant to a necklace.

A **pin back** has a flat front with several holes through which you can secure it to a piece of beadwork. The back of the pin has a sharp wire with a lever catch to keep it closed.

■ *Stringing materials*

Many of the necklaces and bracelets in these projects are made with some kind of stringing material. Here's a list of the stringing supplies you'll need.

Beading thread is a very pliable thread made of nylon. It's fairly strong and comes in dozens of colors. Some beading threads come pre-waxed, but if yours isn't, coat it liberally with wax or thread conditioner.

Beading needles are extremely thin pieces of stiff wire (about the width of a piece of thread) that have a tiny hole on one end and a very sharp point on the other. The most popular for beading include English beading needles, which are especially thin and long, and sharp needles, which have a stronger body and are somewhat shorter.

Less stiff than nylon beading thread, **beading floss** is available at most craft stores. It's stretchy, but very strong.

Monofilament is a tough, synthetic material developed by the fishing industry. It's available in a clear version that's very popular with jewelry designers. It's fairly stiff, so you don't need to use a beading needle while working with it.

Leather and hemp are decorative cords that add wonderful texture to any design. Both are strong and durable—perfect for projects that require sturdy stringing material.

Beads

Beads come in an astounding array of types and colors. They're usually measured in millimeters, with the size referring to the diameter of the bead. The beads listed below are used in this book.

Seed beads are small glass beads made by cutting long, thin tubes of glass into tiny pieces. The most common sizes are between 6° and 14° (largest to smallest), and they come in an enormous array of colors.

Composed of glass, **fire-polished beads** are passed through a flame or tumbled, which gives them a smooth, glistening appearance.

Freshwater pearl beads are created naturally by freshwater mollusks. They come in a variety of colors and shapes.

Metal beads are simply beads made out of metal. They come in precious and base metal varieties, including sterling silver, gold-filled, and silver- and gold-plated.

Basic Crochet Stitches

If you're wondering how many yo's to make for a double crochet cluster, you're in the right place. Here you'll find step-by-step, illustrated explanations for all of the stitches used to create the jewelry in this book. You'll also find explanations for out-of-the-ordinary stitches and techniques you may need, including traditional Irish crochet, beaded crochet, and tapestry crochet.

Chain stitch

The chain stitch (ch) is the basis for all crochet projects. Practically every crochet pattern starts with a series of chain stitches that's called a foundation row. Once you've completed the foundation row of chain stitches, you'll add more rows or rounds (rnds) to the project.

To begin your first chain stitch, make a slip-knot on the hook. While holding the hook, bring the yarn over the hook from back to front. Then bring the yarn through the loop on the hook and let the loop slip off the hook. Your first chain stitch is complete.

To make a row of chain stitches, repeat these steps. As you add to the row, bring the thumb and middle finger of your yarn hand—the hand that isn't holding the hook—up to hold the chain (figure 1). To make sure the chain isn't too tight, work your stitches on the widest section of the hook. As you work, try to maintain an even tension in the yarn and to make even stitches.

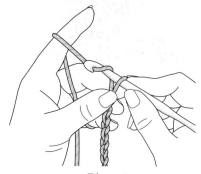

Figure 1

Single crochet

The single crochet (sc) stitch is a short stitch that's fundamental to just about any crochet project.

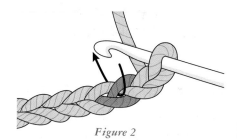

Figure 2

1 To work a row of single crochet stitches, start with a foundation chain of any number of stitches. Count two chain stitches down from the crochet hook, then insert the hook beneath the two top loops of this chain stitch (figure 2).

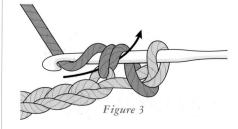

Figure 3

2 Carry the yarn over the hook, catch the yarn, and pull it through the loop on the hook (figure 3). You should have two loops on your hook at this point.

3 To complete your first single crochet stitch, bring the yarn over the hook one more time, grab the yarn with the hook, and

pull the yarn through both of the loops (figure 4). Then insert the hook into the next chain stitch and follow the same steps to make another single crochet (figure 5).

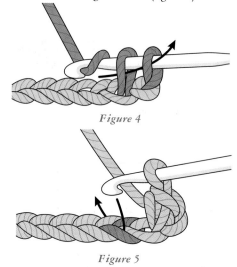

Figure 4

Figure 5

Double crochet

The double crochet (dc) stitch is twice the length of the single crochet stitch. When combined with other stitches, the double crochet stitch can be used to make different textures and patterns in crochet.

1 To make a double crochet stitch, start with a foundation chain of any number of stitches. Carry the yarn over the hook and insert the hook in the fourth chain down from the hook (figure 6).

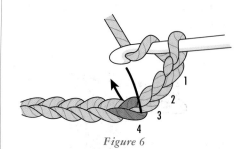

Figure 6

2 Bring the yarn over the hook again and pull the yarn through the chain stitch. At this point, you should have three loops on your hook (figure 7).

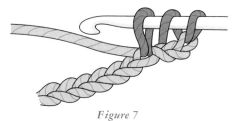

Figure 7

3 Bring the yarn over the hook once more and pull the yarn through the first two loops on the hook, so that you have two loops on your hook (figure 8).

Figure 8

4 Bring the yarn over the hook again and pull the yarn through the remaining two loops on your hook (figure 9). Your first double crochet stitch is now complete. Only one loop should be left on your hook at this point, so that you can begin your next double crochet stitch.

Figure 9

5 To continue, bring the yarn over the hook, insert the hook in the next stitch and continue working across the row (figure 10). When you reach the end of the row, turn your work and chain three to make your turning chain.

Figure 10

Half double crochet

The half double crochet (hdc) is used frequently in crochet patterns. It's slightly shorter than a double crochet and taller than a single crochet. To start, make a foundation chain of any number of stitches.

1 Bring the yarn over the hook, locate the third chain stitch from the hook (figure 11), and insert the hook in the chain.

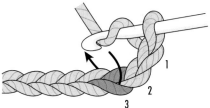

Figure 11

2 Bring the yarn over the hook and catch it with the hook. Pull the hook through the chain. You should have three loops on the hook (figure 12).

Figure 12

3 Bring the yarn over the hook, catch the yarn with the hook, and pull it through the three loops on the hook (figure 13).

Figure 13

4 You will have one loop left on the hook. You've created one half double crochet stitch (figure 14). Yarn over and insert the hook in the next chain and repeat the sequence across the row.

Figure 14

Treble or triple crochet

Treble crochet or triple crochet (tr) is taller than double crochet. It's often used to create an open, lacey fabric. Start with a foundation chain of any number of stitches.

1 Identify the fifth chain stitch from the hook. Bring the yarn over the hook twice (figure 15).

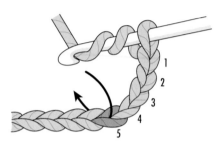

Figure 15

2 Insert the hook into the fifth chain. Bring the yarn over the hook, catch the yarn, and pull the hook through the chain. You'll have four loops on the hook (figure 16).

Figure 16

3 Bring the yarn over the hook, catch the yarn, and slide the hook through the first two loops (figure 17).

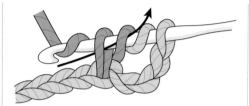

Figure 17

4 Yarn over the hook and draw your yarn through the next two loops on the hook (figure 18).

Figure 18

5 Yarn over the hook and draw the yarn through the last two loops on your hook (figure 19).

Figure 19

6 You will end up with only one loop on your hook. You've completed one treble crochet stitch (figure 20). Yarn over twice and repeat the steps in the next chain stitch.

Figure 20

Slip stitch

The slip stitch (sl st) is used frequently in crochet and serves a wide variety of purposes. You can use it to finish an edge or to connect two separate pieces of crochet. You can also use it to add a new skein of yarn to a project. The slip stitch is most frequently used to connect one end of a foundation chain to the other end of the chain, making a ring. The ring is then used as a foundation for crocheting pieces in the round.

To make a slip stitch, insert the hook into any designated stitch, then bring the yarn over, catch the yarn, and pull the hook through the stitch and through the loop on your hook. This completes one slip stitch. You should have one loop left on the hook (figure 21).

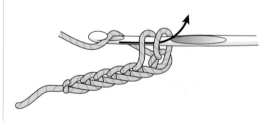

Figure 21

Special Techniques and Stitches

The following stitches are not used in every project but are useful to know and fun to experiment with. If the pattern you're working requires any of these special stitches, be sure to turn to this section.

Picot

The picot stitch (no abbreviation) is a round stitch used to embellish an edge or fill an empty gap in a mesh pattern. Picots come in different sizes. A definition for a specific picot used in a project will be provided with the pattern. To make a standard chain-3 picot stitch, do the following.

1 Chain 3, then insert the hook in the third chain from the hook (figure 22) and yarn over.

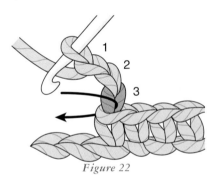

Figure 22

2 Draw the yarn through the stitch and through the loop on the hook (figure 23).

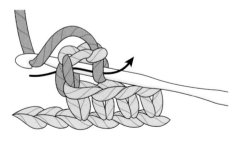

Figure 23

Knot stitch (knot st)

This special stitch is simply a lengthened chain stitch locked in place with a single crochet stitch worked into the back loop.

1 Draw up a loop as directed in your pattern. Wrap the yarn over your hook (figure 24).

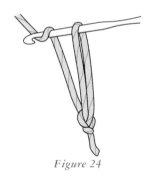

Figure 24

2 Pull the yarn through the hook (elongated chain stitch made). Grasp the two front threads of your chain with your fingers, separating them from the back thread (figure 25).

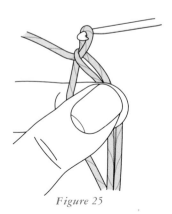

Figure 25

3 Position the hook under the single thread and bring the thread over the hook (figure 26).

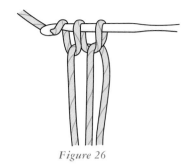

Figure 26

4 Draw the yarn through and bring the thread over once more (figure 27).

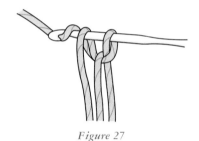

Figure 27

5 Draw both loops on the hook to complete the stitch (1 knot stitch made) (figure 28).

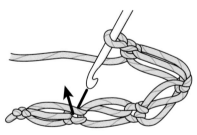

Figure 28

Working around a ring

Crocheting around a center ring is as easy as working in rows. When you work in the round, you'll need to increase the number of stitches per row so that you can go around the growing circumference of the circle. Most patterns will indicate the number of stitches required for each round of the pattern.

To work around a ring, you should make a center ring as a foundation for your stitches. You can do this by making a chain of any number of stitches and then connecting the two ends of the chain with a slip stitch.

1 Create the center ring by first making a chain with the number of stitches specified in your pattern. In this example, it's a chain of six (figure 29).

Figure 29

2 Insert your hook into the first chain and bring the yarn over the hook (figure 30).

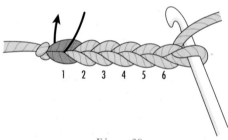

Figure 30

3 Pull the yarn through the stitch and the loop on your hook to complete the foundation ring (figure 31).

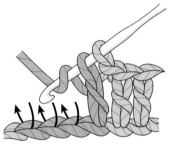

Figure 31

Once the ring is complete, you can work your first round. Your first stitches should be made into the center of the ring. (If you're making a tube form, you'll work into the foundation chain stitches rather than the round itself.) If your piece is worked in a spiral, you should mark the beginning of each round with a stitch marker, so that you'll be able to tell where one round begins or ends.

Cluster

The cluster stitch (no abbreviation) is made up of a number of half-closed stitches (the number of which will be stated in the pattern) worked across an equal number of stitches and joined at the top. The example shows how to make a cluster with four double crochet stitches.

1 Yarn over, insert the hook into the next stitch, yarn over, draw the yarn through the stitch, yarn over, and draw the yarn through the two loops on the hook.

2 Repeat step 1 three times (figure 32).

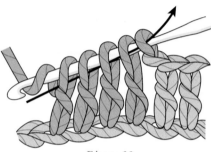

Figure 32

3 Yarn over and draw the yarn through all five loops on the hook (figure 33).

Figure 33

Figure 34 shows a finished 4–double crochet cluster stitch.

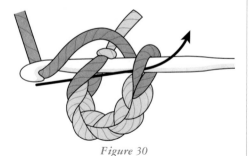

Figure 34

Puff stitch

The puff stitch (puff st) makes a gently puffed oval shape. The creation of a puff stitch is similar to that of the cluster stitch in that you half-close several stitches worked in the same stitch and then join them at the top to complete the stitch.

1 Yarn over, insert the hook in the next stitch, yarn over, pull the yarn through the stitch, yarn over, and draw the yarn through the two loops on the hook. Two loops remain on the hook (figure 35).

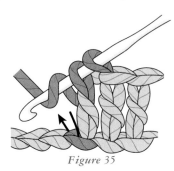

Figure 35

2 In the same stitch, repeat step 1 twice. You should have four loops on your hook.

3 Yarn over and draw the yarn through all four loops on the hook (figure 36). See figure 37 for a complete puff stitch.

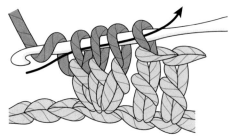

Figure 36

Figure 37

Bobble stitch

The bobble stitch (no abbreviation) is made with a series of loops instead of stitches. It produces an oval bump that's smooth, and it works best with yarn of a heavier weight.

1 Yarn over and insert the hook in the stitch (figure 38).

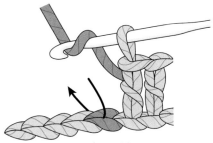

Figure 38

2 Yarn over and draw the yarn through the stitch, bringing the loop up to the height of the previous stitch. You should have three loops on the hook (figure 39).

Figure 39

3 Working in the same stitch, repeat steps 1 and 2 four times. You should have 11 loops on the hook.

4 Yarn over and draw the yarn though all 11 loops on the hook (figure 40). One bobble is now complete (figure 41).

Figure 40

Figure 41

Irish crochet

Traditionally executed with very fine cotton thread, Irish crochet dates back to the nineteenth century. The technique is used to produce pieces with a delicate, lacy look. Most Irish crochet projects are made up of a combination of individual motifs that are worked separately, then connected by a mesh background. Common motifs include roses, leaves, clover, and honeycombs.

Clones knot

The Clones knot (no abbreviation) is a stitch frequently used in Irish crochet. It can be worked off a chain or a single crochet. Here, a Clones knot is worked off a chain.

1 Make one chain, yarn over, then pass the hook downward under the chain, and catch up a loop. Bring the loop forward and up, and yarn over again, as if for a treble crochet. Continue to catch up loops from over and under the chain, doing so the number of times specified in your pattern—usually about 16 loops for fine thread (figure 42).

Figure 42

2 Draw through all the loops on the hook at once, yarn over, and draw through the loop on the hook.

3 Make a slip stitch around the chain at the base of the knot, drawing tightly. You should make the knot even and rather loose (figure 43).

Figure 43

Tapestry crochet

The tapestry crochet technique can be used to produce colorful patterns and motifs that look like woven tapestries. The patterns are usually charted on graph paper and worked in rows of very tight stitches. When making a tapestry crochet project, you'll use two or more different colors of yarn at the same time. One yarn is worked, while the other yarn is carried. Stiffer

material is often used in tapestry crochet, usually a sport-weight cotton yarn. The sturdy yarn allows you to reproduce the feeling of a thick tapestry in your work. Keep in mind that when you're working with thicker yarn, you'll want to use a larger hook.

Before you begin your tapestry crochet project, make sure that all of the yarns you're using are of the same weight. If you mix thin yarn with thicker yarn, your pattern will look distorted.

Inserting the hook

Once the initial row or round of stitches is complete, you should insert your hook from front to back, beneath the top two loops of the stitch you're working into. Make sure the front of the piece is facing you.

Carrying the yarn

Carrying different colors of yarn is a critical part of tapestry crochet. The hidden yarns give the project extra texture and make it stiff. By carrying yarns, you'll also avoid knots and loose ends.

To carry a yarn, lay the yarn across the top two loops of the stitches you're working into, leaving a one-inch tail of the new yarn in the back (figure 44). You can hold

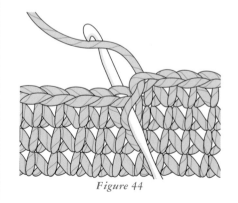

Figure 44

the carried yarn in place with the thumb of your left hand. Then single crochet across the row, making sure the carried yarn stays on top of the loops. Crochet around the carried yarn (figure 45). Your work should be tight, so that the carried yarn can't be seen from the front or back. Once you've finished the row, you can cut off the tail on the back of the piece.

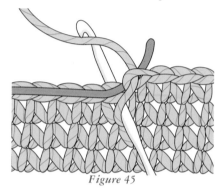

Figure 45

If you want to create a tapestry motif with a number of different hues, you can carry more than one color of yarn at the same time. Remember that each yarn you carry will make your crochet stitch taller. To create a neat, uniform motif, carry your yarn or yarns at the very start of the project, even if you won't be changing colors right away. It's best to carry only two or three different yarns at a time. If you carry too many strands at once, you'll have a tangle of yarn on your hands.

Making the tapestry crochet stitch

The tapestry crochet stitch is very much like the single crochet stitch, except that yarns are carried as the working yarn is crocheted around them. To work the tapestry crochet stitch:

1 Change yarns when two loops of an incomplete single crochet stitch are on your hook.

2 Yarn over with the carried yarn and pull it through both of the loops on your hook. Then single crochet across the row with the new yarn and carry the old yarn until you're ready to switch colors again.

Tip: Before your working yarn runs out, carry a new piece of yarn five or more stitches prior to working it. Then change to the new yarn and carry the tail of the old yarn five or more stitches to make sure it's secure.

Counting stitches and checking the gauge

The tapestry stitch is V-shaped, with two loops at the top that also make a V. To count tapestry crochet stitches, you should count the Vs in the body of the pattern. You can also count the V loops at the top.

Use a ruler to check your stitches per inch. Put the ruler in a position parallel to the rows, then line up an inch marker between two of the stitches. Count the number of stitches between the inch marker you lined up and the next inch marker. To check the rows, lay a ruler in a position perpendicular to the rows. Then line up an inch marker between two of the rows and count the rows in between the marker you lined up and the next inch marker.

Crocheting with beads

Beads can make any piece of crocheted jewelry or fabric extra-special. Two different techniques for crocheting beads into your project are shown below.

Pre-stringing

This method is perfect for projects that require a specific number of beads. Just string the beads onto your ball of yarn before you start crocheting. Then slide a bead up the yarn whenever you want to add it to a stitch.

Before you begin, make sure you're working with beads that have holes big enough for your yarn to fit through. String the number of beads required for your project onto the yarn. For easy stringing, thread your yarn through a beading needle that has a large eye, then string your beads onto the yarn.

To work a bead into a stitch, make the stitch, but stop when one step is left in completing it and there are two loops on your hook. Then move one of the beads up so that it's near the stitch, carry the yarn over, and finish the stitch in the normal fashion (figure 46). The bead should be on the side of the project that's facing away from you. If you want to add a bead to the side of the project that's facing you, move the bead completely up prior to inserting your hook and starting the stitch.

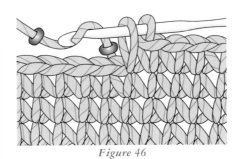

Figure 46

Adding individual beads

Incorporating beads one at a time while you're working your stitches gives you a bit of creative freedom in terms of the design of your project. If you don't know the precise number of beads you'll use or

exactly where you want to put the beads in the project, this method of adding as you go works well.

To use this technique, you'll need beads with center holes that are big enough to hold two separate strands of your yarn. You'll also need a steel hook with a fine gauge. Once you have a loop on your working hook, put a bead on the shaft of the steel hook and move the loop from your working hook to the steel hook. Then slide the bead over the loop, so that the bead is at the base of the loop, and the loop is strung through the top of the bead. Pull enough yarn through so that the working hook will fit in the loop above the bead and insert your hook. Then finish the stitch in the normal fashion.

Sewing with beads

To sew beads onto a completed crochet piece, you'll need a needle and thread. This method is ideal if you're working with fragile beads, or if you've already completed your project and want to jazz it up a bit. When selecting thread for sewing the beads, pick a type that goes well with your yarn. As you sew, be sure to stitch through the actual yarn rather than around the crochet stitches.

Tip: Make a gauge swatch before you start your actual project! The use of beads will alter the elasticity and shape of your crochet fabric and add weight to the project. Be sure to play around with the swatch prior to embarking on the actual piece.

Basic Shaping Techniques

Working only a rectangle or circle of crochet could be mind-numbing and not very useful. There are only so many things you can do with either of those shapes. Simply by adding or subtracting the number of stitches in a row, you can shape the fabric you're creating. It's very important to count stitches as you increase or decrease according to your pattern. Take time to count your stitches, and then count them again!

Increasing

Increasing stitches are simply added stitches worked into a row. Your pattern will tell you when and where to increase (inc). It may be at the beginning, end, or even the middle of the row you're working on. No matter where the increase appears, simply working a given number of stitches into one stitch makes an increase.

Working an increase at the beginning or end of a row is the most common method to add stitches; it gives your fabric a smooth edge. In the example shown, a double crochet increase is worked into the first stitch (figure 47). (Remember: Your turning chain counts as the first stitch!) Figure 48 illustrates a double crochet increase in the middle of a row.

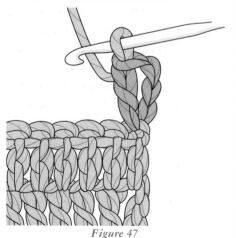

Figure 47

Figure 48

Decreasing

Decreasing is simply subtracting stitches. A decrease (dec) can be worked at the beginning, end, or middle of a row. Your pattern will tell you precisely where and how to make a decrease. In short, you combine two separate stitches into one stitch.

Read your pattern directions carefully so you understand how to work decreases successfully.

For a decrease in double crochet (also called a two double crochet cluster or dc2tog), work a double crochet until you have two loops on your hook. Yarn over your hook and insert it in the next stitch. Yarn over, draw the yarn through the stitch, yarn over and draw the yarn through the first two loops on your hook. Yarn over and draw the yarn through all three loops on your hook.

In the example shown (figure 49), a decrease has been worked in double crochet. If you look at the tops of the stitches, you will see only one stitch crossing the top of two stitch posts.

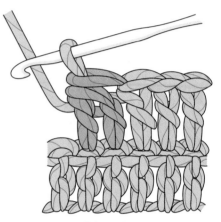

Figure 49

Additional Techniques

Along with basic crochet techniques, there are a few craft and jewelry-making procedures you'll need to familiarize yourself with in order to make the projects in this book.

Working with wire

Loops and links made of wire hold many of these projects together, so becoming proficient at wire bending is a must. Don't despair if your results look less than spectacular at first—making attractive loops and links really is just a matter of practice.

Wire loops come in two versions, simple and wrapped.

To make a simple loop

1 Use needle-nose pliers to make a 90° bend ⅜"/10mm from the end of the wire; or, if you're using the loop to secure a bead, cut the wire ⅜"/10mm from the top of the bead and make the 90° bend right at the top of the bead (figure 50).

Figure 50

2 Use round-nose pliers to grasp the wire end and roll the pliers until the wire touches the 90° bend (figure 51).

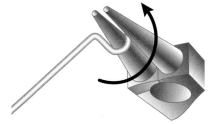

Figure 51

To make a wrapped loop

1 Use needle-nose pliers to make a 90° bend in the wire about 2"/5cm from one wire end. Then use round-nose pliers to grasp the bend, shape the wire over the top jaw, and swing it underneath to form a partial loop (figure 52).

Figure 52

2 Use needle-nose pliers or your fingers to wrap the wire in a tight coil down the stem. Then trim the excess wire close to the wrap and use needle-nose pliers to tighten the wire end (figure 53).

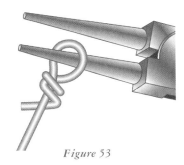

Figure 53

Opening a jump ring

Never open a jump ring by pulling the ends apart to make the circle larger—this will distort the shape of the ring and weaken the wire. Instead, use two pairs of pliers to grip the ring on either side of the split. Then gently pull one side away from you and the other side toward you, add your bead or clasp, and close the ring by reversing the motion.

Felting

Felting occurs when an item made of wool is forced to shrink, fuzz up, and become felt. The transformation takes place when the wool piece is treated with hot water, soap, and agitation. This causes the individual wool fibers to become tangled and intertwined, so that they form the dense, matted fabric known as felt. The effect can be achieved through hand- or machine-washing. For the felted projects in this book, you can use your washing machine.

To felt in the washing machine

Place the project to be felted in a mesh bag and drop the bag into the washing machine along with something that will create extra friction—preferably a light-colored item, like a white canvas bag, that won't bleed or produce lint. Then add about 1 Tbsp/15mL of liquid dish soap and set the machine for a hot water wash using the lowest water level possible. The low water level will create more friction. Once the wash cycle gets underway, check every five or 10 minutes to see how the item is felting. When fully felted, the piece should be roughly one-third smaller than when you started. Once the project has felted sufficiently, rinse it by hand with cold water and wrap it in a towel. Press down gently on the towel to squeeze out any excess water, then let the item air-dry.

Stiffening

Fabric stiffener is a liquid substance that adds body to fabric. There are many brands available. To use it, you'll need a bowl that's large enough to hold your project. Pour enough stiffener into the bowl to completely cover the project and work the stiffener into the fabric until it's saturated. Then take the project out and squeeze out any excess liquid. Arrange the project into the desired shape and let it air-dry. For small projects, or items that don't need a lot of extra body, you can thin the stiffener by mixing it with water.

Knotting

To make an overhand knot, form a loop with the yarn, passing the yarn end through the loop and pulling tight (figure 54).

Figure 54

Make a square knot by first forming an overhand knot, right end over left end, and finish with another overhand knot, this time left end over right end (figure 55).

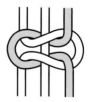

Figure 55

Reading a Pattern

We hope you've flipped through this book and been inspired to make every project in it! To get started, all you need to do is gather the materials and follow the pattern instructions.

Written patterns give you a lot of important information before you actually pick up your hook and yarn. Reading a pattern from beginning to end before you crochet isn't an optional step; it's required, and simply makes sense. Even experienced crocheters do it. Think of it as if you were sitting down with a road atlas before embarking on a long road trip: It's easy to map out where you're going and how to get there before you leave the house—a whole lot easier than attempting to whip out the map and read it in eight lanes of speeding, rush hour traffic in a strange city!

Let's take a look at what you can expect to learn from crochet patterns in this book or any other book or magazine.

Experience Level

A pattern will tell you which level of experience it's designed for: beginner, easy, intermediate, or experienced. Pay attention to the level of experience needed to create a project, then read through the pattern just to be sure it's right for you.

Beginners will use basic stitches in a straightforward manner. There will be minimal shaping of the project.

Easy patterns use basic stitches, simple repetitive stitch patterns, simple color changes, and easy-to-master shaping and finishing techniques.

Intermediate patterns use a variety of stitches and more complex stitch patterns. Lace patterns and complex color changes may also be used.

Experienced level patterns will use intricate stitch patterns, work from charted stitches, use finer threads, smaller hooks, and detailed shaping and finishing.

Size or Dimensions

A pattern will give you the finished dimensions of a project or provide you with the size ranges that can be made with the pattern.

Materials and Tools

Every pattern will list the materials, the specific hook size, and other tools that you'll need. The pattern will tell you exactly which type of yarn is used and approximately how much you'll need to create the project. In most cases, the pattern will tell you the specific brand of yarn used to crochet the project.

Stitch List

The stitches used in the pattern will be listed. If advanced or specialty stitches are used, you'll be given directions for the stitches. These stitches will be listed in abbreviated form to save space (see chart on page 127). If special changes in standard stitch construction or unique working methods are used, those changes will be noted and brought to your attention before you start.

Gauge

A gauge will be specified for the design. Pay attention to the gauge. If you want your project to be the size you intend it to be, make a gauge sample before you start on the project.

Gauge is measured by stitches or rows of stitches per inch. If your project is made solely with single crochet, you'll use single crochet stitches to make the sample. If the project has a set of several different stitches that repeat across the row, you'll need to create a sample for that set of stitches.

Create a gauge sample that measures 4 x 4 inches (10 x 10 cm) or larger. It's imperative that you create your sample with the same yarn and hook you plan to use to crochet the project.

If your sample doesn't result in the specified gauge, rework another sample with a larger (or smaller) hook size or adjust your stitch tension as you crochet until your sample matches the required gauge. It's as simple as that.

Instructions, Pattern Notes, and Graphs

Every pattern will be written with step-by-step instructions for each and every row you crochet. (Really.) It will begin with the number of chain stitches you need for your foundation row, then continue with a row-by-row description of the stitches or pattern stitches needed to complete the project. If the project is made with several pieces, each piece will be given separate step-by-step directions.

If there are special stitch variations or unusual working methods for the pattern, these will be noted in a separate section of pattern notes or working notes.

If there are specific color changes that make up a pattern for checks or stripes, these changes may be shown graphically with an illustration or a charted graph. Each square on a charted graph will be equal to a given number of stitches.

When a garment is made up of one or more pieces, you may be given a diagram that shows the dimensions of each piece needed to create the project.

Finishing and Assembly

Finally, if your project needs to be blocked (shaped) or assembled, the instructions will tell you what to do and, in some cases, how to do it.

In addition, if the project calls for buttonholes, fringe, pompoms, or other embellishments you'll be given instructions on how to create each one as needed.

Substituting Fibers

If you don't like the particular shade of green used in a choker pattern, or you're allergic to the mohair yarn that's called for in a certain project, don't worry! You shouldn't feel constrained by a designer's selection of color or fiber. You can substitute the yarn of your choice for the same type of yarn called for in the pattern. Simply follow the four steps below to substitute the yarn of your choice.

1 Identify the yarn type that the pattern calls for. Yarn companies classify each of their yarns by weight or size (yarn thickness). There's some crossover between types, but in general, they're separated into six distinct groups: superfine yarns, fine yarns, light yarns, medium weight yarns, bulky, and super bulky yarns.

Once you know the type of yarn you need, look for a similar type of yarn that suits your needs and desires. Most—if not all—yarns have the yarn type printed on the label. But don't go shopping yet.

2 Determine how much yarn the project requires. Jot down the total length of each ball of the original yarn in the pattern. Multiply the number of balls called for by yards/meters per ball. This will tell you how much yarn you will need. Write down the total amount of each yarn type you will need for the project.

3 Here's the fun part—go to your local yarn shop, craft store, or visit the myriad of yarn suppliers online. When you find the yarn you want to use, divide the total yardage you need by the yards/meters per ball of your new yarn. Round up to the next whole number (you don't want to run short of yarn!). This will give you the number of skeins you'll need of the substitute yarn.

4 Finally, crochet a gauge sample with the recommended hook and the yarn you've purchased. Don't skip this step. If the gauge is accurate, crochet away!

Finishing Touches

You've made your very last stitch in a project, but you're not finished yet! As you look at your finished piece you'll see that edges may be curled or the piece is slightly misshapen. Here are the techniques you'll need to finish off your project.

Fastening Off

When you've come to the end of your pattern and made your very last stitch, you'll need to cut your skein of yarn from the crocheted fabric. If you don't fasten the yarn properly, the sight of unraveling stitches will dismay you.

Cut the yarn about 6"/15cm from the hook. Draw the end of the yarn through the last loop on your hook. Pull the tail of the yarn gently to tighten the loop. This will prevent the accidental unraveling of your stitches.

Weaving in the End(s)

Thread a large-eyed tapestry needle with the tail of your yarn end. Weave the yarn through three or four stitches. To secure the weaving, weave back through the same stitches. Cut the yarn close to—but not up against—the crocheted fabric. Gently pull the fabric, and the yarn end will disappear into the stitches.

Weave in other yarn ends that you have on the wrong side of your fabric in the same way.

Blocking

As you crochet the piece you are working on, it may become a little misshapen. It may not look like a perfect rectangle, precisely match the dimensions of the pattern, or the edges may be curled. Don't panic. All that's needed is a little gentle persuasion, a process known as blocking. With very few tools and a little effort, you can block an item to the shape that is desired or needed.

First and foremost, you'll need a flat, padded surface to work on. Some good choices: an ironing board, a mattress in the guest room, or a large piece of heavy cardboard slipped inside a large plastic trash bag. The size of your project will dictate the size of padded surface you need. Cover any flat surface with a sheet of plastic or a large trash bag to prevent moisture from damaging the surface. If needed, use a stack of several absorbent bath towels to pad your flat surface. You'll need the padding in order to stick pins into the padded surface to hold your work.

In addition to a flat surface to work on, you'll need the following simple tools to steam or spray block an item:

Rust-proof T-pins or straight pins
Steam iron
Spray bottle
Tape measure or ruler

Steam Blocking

Steam blocking is used to lightly block an item that has curling edges or one that is slightly misshapen.

1 Set your iron to a temperature that is compatible with the fiber content of your yarn. If in doubt about the fiber content, use a medium-low setting.

2 Lay your item flat on a padded surface. Lightly tug at the item to bring it into the shape desired. Use pins to hold the item to the desired shape on the padded surface. Check your measurements with a tape measure if needed.

3 Hold your heated steam iron about an inch above the fabric and steam the item. Don't press the iron on the fabric!

4 Allow the item to cool and dry completely before removing the pins.

Spray Blocking

Spray blocking is a little more time-consuming than steam blocking (it takes longer to dry). It's useful if your item is more than a bit misshapen.

1 Lay your item flat on a moisture-protected, padded surface.

2 Gently stretch your item to conform to the correct shape or measurements. Pin the item in place with rust-proof pins.

3 Fill a clean spray bottle with lukewarm water. Spritz the item until it is slightly damp; don't soak it.

4 Smooth the fabric with your hands and pin it with additional pins if the edges are wavy.

5 Allow the crocheted item to dry completely before you remove the pins.

Crochet Hook Sizes

Continental	U.S.
2.25 mm	B-1
2.75 mm	C-2
3.25 mm	D-3
3.5 mm	E-4
3.75 mm	F-5
4 mm	G-6
4.5 mm	7
5 mm	H-8
5.5 mm	I-9
6 mm	J-10
6.5 mm	K-10½
8 mm	L-11
9 mm	M/N-13
10 mm	N/P-15
15 mm	P/Q
16 mm	Q
19 mm	S

★ Letter or number may vary by manufacturer. For accurate and consistent sizing, rely on the millimeter (mm) size.

Steel Crochet Hook Sizes

Continental	U. S.
2.7 mm	00
2.55 mm	0
2.35 mm	1
2.2 mm	2
2 mm	3
1.75 mm	4
1.7 mm	5
1.6 mm	6
1.5 mm	7
1.4 mm	8
1.25 mm	9
1.15 mm	10
1.05 mm	11
1 mm	12
.95 mm	13
.90 mm	14

Abbreviations

alt	alternate
Alt lp st	alternate loop stitch
approx	approximately
bsc	bead single crochet
beg	begin, beginning
bet	between
BL	back loop
BP	back post
ch	chain
ch-sp	chain space
cont	continue
dc	double crochet
dec	decrease(s/ing)
dtr	double treble crochet
ea	each
esc	extended single crochet
FL	front loop
FP	front post
hdc	half double crochet
hk	hook
inc	increase(s/ing)
knot st	knot stitch
lp(s)	loop(s)
oz	ounce(s)
patt	pattern
prev	previous
puff st	puff stitch
rem	remaining
rep	repeat
reverse sc	reverse single crochet
RS	right side
rnd(s)	round(s)
sc	single crochet
sk	skip
sl st	slip stitch
sp(s)	space(s)
st(s)	stitches
tch	turning chain
tog	together
tr	treble crochet
WS	wrong side
yo	yarn over

Designers

Vashti Braha currently serves on the board of directors for the Crochet Guild of America (CGOA). Her designs can be found in various crochet books, magazines, and the CGOA Pattern Line. When she's not busy exploring crochet's limitless potential, Vashti maintains her blog, designingvashti.blogspot.com, meets as many crocheters as possible at CGOA conferences and online, and helps her young son design his own quirky toys.

Veena Burry has been enthusiastic about fiber arts—especially knitting, crocheting, and weaving—since early childhood. She has taught extensively and led fiber arts workshops. Her web site, www.knittingguru.com, features knitting and crochet tips, as well as kits, custom-made garments, and accessories. Veena lives in New York City and draws inspiration from gardening, and from trips with her husband to the opera, theater, concerts, and museums.

Alexandra Calub, known to friends as Alie, lives and crochets in the Philippines. The art of crochet, which she learned from her grandmother and mother, has been a hobby since she was ten years old. Alie now runs a small crochet business out of her home. She designs and creates original crocheted items, including home accents and fashion accessories, and all products are produced through livelihood projects with poor urban women. Her designs can be seen at www.crochetbyalie.com.

Kelly Farrell received a B.F. A. in metalsmithing from Virginia Commonwealth Universtiy. Her art studio is tucked in the corner of a vintage motorscooter shop in Richmond, Virginia. In addition to creating her own work, Kelly runs a handmade craft boutique called Dada Haus, which promotes the work of talented artisans. Kelly, who has appeared on the DIY Network show *Craft Lab*, is an active member of the indie craft scene, running an online directory of alternative craft shows and participating in her local Craft Mafia. More of Kelly's work is available at www.fishtop.com and www.dadahaus.com.

Paula Gron lives with her sculptor husband, Jack, and their cat in Corpus Christi, Texas. She made her first craft project—a saddle created out of newspaper and rope for a bronco-busting seat on a porch rail—at the age of eight. Paula is now an award-winning graphic designer and commercial illustrator. Through her crochet projects, she is able to combine her design background with her long-time love of crafting.

Gwen Blakley Kinsler is the founder and past president of the CGOA. She has published articles on needlework and her own crochet design patterns. She is a Certified Craft Yarn Council of America Instructor and is committed to the importance of sharing her passion for crochet with anyone interested in learning, especially children. She is the co-author of *Crocheting—Kids Can Do It* (Kids Can Press, 2003).

Marty Miller lives and teaches in Greensboro, North Carolina. She has been crocheting and creating her own patterns since she was a little girl. Her designs have appeared in magazines, books, and fashion shows. She is a professional member and the Mentor Coordinator of the CGOA. When she isn't crocheting or designing, Marty serves as an exercise instructor and personal trainer at a local health club.

Elizabeta Nedeljkovich-Martonosi is an ex-Yugoslav doctor, who came to the United States to see her daughters through college. She now practices all types of needlecraft, from sewing, knitting, and crochet to acupuncture. While she enjoys designing imaginative garments, Elizabeta's main interest is crocheted jewelry. She also speaks four languages and does work in polymer clay and metal. Elizabeta has two shops on the web: JewelLace.etsy.com, and beta-fashions.com.

Designers

MaryKate Newcomb learned how to crochet from her stern, third-grade teacher. Crochet is now her main creative outlet. MaryKate teaches art lessons in her home, enjoys photographing her extensive Smurf collection, and listening to audiobooks. She lives in Baltimore, Maryland, with her husband and son. Her blog is www.ganap.com/blog.html.

Lindsay Obermeyer lives in Chicago, Illinois. Her grandmother taught her to knit and crochet. Lindsay teaches and has lectured extensively on the topics of fiber arts and needlecraft. She holds an M.F.A. from the University of Washington, an M.A.T. from National-Louis University, and a B.F.A. from the School of the Art Institute of Chicago. Her work has been shown in Boston's Museum of Fine Arts and the Milwaukee Art Museum, and can be viewed on her web site, www.lbostudio.com

Jessica Schleicher specializes in crochet jewelry and pattern design. She is the creator and owner of Knot By Gran'ma, an online boutique. Each piece of Jessica's jewelry is one of a kind, created by using a variety of crochet and jewelry-making techniques. Jessica's patterns are all inspired by original pieces of art, which she created herself. Knot By Gran'ma jewelry and patterns can be found at www.knotbygranma.com.

Severina is the corset-wearing alter-ego of designer **Aundrea Murphy**. Severina obsesses over all things vintage and specializes in reproducing clothing using antique needlework and sewing patterns. Her patterns and designs are featured on her blog: vintagestitchorama.blogspot.com.

Pam Shore learned to crochet at the age of 12. Inspired by the resurgence of crochet in the 1970s, her addiction to the art progressed rapidly, as did her collection of hooks and books. Since 1995, the CGOA, with its annual conferences and internet crochet groups, has fueled her creativity by exposing her to many other passionate crocheters and fiber artists. Pam will be eternally grateful to the CGOA!

Lindsay Streem lives in Chicago, Illinois, with her husband and an ever-growing collection of yarn. She has been crafting since she was a young girl in Missouri, when she created her first purple ribbon afghan for a county fair. These days, she enjoys creating stylish accessories, including cool crocheted jewelry and housewares. Lindsay is inspired by anything vintage, especially old magazines and patterns. Her designs are available online at www.crochetgirl.etsy.com.

Nicole Tirona grew up in San Francisco and Manila. She's currently pursuing a degree in Visual Arts at the Emily Carr Institute of Art and Design in Vancouver, British Columbia. Nicole is addicted to making art and crafts, and especially enjoys designing jewelry and other accessories. Her work is featured on two web sites: nicoletirona.blogspot.com and itsyourlife.etsy.com.

While serving as a Peace Corps volunteer in highland Guatemala in the 1970s, **Carol Ventura** was inspired by the colorful tapestry crocheted shoulder bags made in the region. She has since explored the design potential of the tapestry crochet technique, developed a system of diagramming patterns, and created a variety of flat and three-dimensional projects, which she has shared in her many publications. For more projects and information about tapestry crochet, visit www.tapestrycrochet.com.

Kelly Wilson loves to create with yarn and beads, and especially enjoys designing jewelry. Kelly's patterns and creations have appeared in pattern booklets and in magazines, such as *Bead Unique, Quick & Easy Crochet,* and *Knit N Style.* Kelly has also appeared on the TV show *Knitty Gritty* on the DIY Network. Her jewelry designs can be found at www.kellywilsondesigns.com, www.anastasiaknits.com, and www.theknittingvault.com.

Index